The Development Dimensions of Trade

OECD

ORGANISATION FOR ECONOMIC CO-OPERATION AND DEVELOPMENT

ORGANISATION FOR ECONOMIC CO-OPERATION AND DEVELOPMENT

Pursuant to Article 1 of the Convention signed in Paris on 14th December 1960, and which came into force on 30th September 1961, the Organisation for Economic Co-operation and Development (OECD) shall promote policies designed:

– to achieve the highest sustainable economic growth and employment and a rising standard of living in Member countries, while maintaining financial stability, and thus to contribute to the development of the world economy;

– to contribute to sound economic expansion in Member as well as non-member countries in the process of economic development; and

– to contribute to the expansion of world trade on a multilateral, non-discriminatory basis in accordance with international obligations.

The original Member countries of the OECD are Austria, Belgium, Canada, Denmark, France, Germany, Greece, Iceland, Ireland, Italy, Luxembourg, the Netherlands, Norway, Portugal, Spain, Sweden, Switzerland, Turkey, the United Kingdom and the United States. The following countries became Members subsequently through accession at the dates indicated hereafter: Japan (28th April 1964), Finland (28th January 1969), Australia (7th June 1971), New Zealand (29th May 1973), Mexico (18th May 1994), the Czech Republic (21st December 1995), Hungary (7th May 1996), Poland (22nd November 1996), Korea (12th December 1996) and the Slovak Republic (14th December 2000). The Commission of the European Communities takes part in the work of the OECD (Article 13 of the OECD Convention).

Publié en français sous le titre :

ÉCHANGES ET DÉVELOPPEMENT : LES ENJEUX

FOREWORD

Any full discussion of trade and development is bound to be multifaceted and potentially quite complex. The expansion of trade opportunities in the years since World War Two played a key role in supporting or even driving development in many countries. The success of trade liberalisation efforts has depended on the establishment of a rules-based multilateral trading system, which was built with tremendous effort and is still evolving. Yet, while there is ample evidence of a strong tendency for a positive association between the openness of an economy and progress on the development front, openness alone is not sufficient to ensure success.

The Development Dimensions of Trade presents the main elements of the relationship between trade and development. It highlights analytically the basis for their positive association and underscores key elements of a policy framework that can enhance this relationship. The study aims to present the evidence in a clear and readable fashion, providing a foundation for future consideration of the issues.

The preparation of the study has benefited from extensive discussion in the OECD's Trade Committee and its Working Party, as well as inputs from other parts of the OECD, particularly the Development Co-operation Directorate. Importantly, non-OECD countries contributed to discussion of the issues and provided constructive comments. The lead drafter of the study was Raed Safadi, with substantial contributions from a number of colleagues. The report is published on the responsibility of the Secretary-General.

TABLE OF CONTENTS

Boxes

Tables and Figures

Chapter I

Chapter II

Chapter IV

Chapter V

APPENDIX 2

EXECUTIVE SUMMARY

Introduction

The central focus of this study is the role of trade and trade policies in development, and the contribution (actual and potential) of the WTO to economic development in non-OECD countries. The study has three main objectives:

1. To foster a better understanding of the links between trade, growth and development.

2. To address the trade concerns and interests of non-OECD countries, and to establish why those interests and concerns are better served within the context of the multilateral trading system. And,

3. To consider how best to provide non-OECD countries with the tools and institutional instruments to better position their public and private sectors to become more fully integrated into the multilateral trading system.

Economic success in non-OECD countries is generally associated with progressive integration into the world economy. Two factors have been particularly important in facilitating integration: 1) domestic reforms to establish framework conditions enabling industries to plug into global production networks; and 2) liberalisation to reduce impediments to the free flow of goods, services and investment across borders. Developing countries that have embraced openness have tended to reap substantial benefits from buoyant world markets; others who failed to do so have tended to see their fortunes stagnate or even decline.

The international trading system has underpinned the integration of non-OECD countries into the world economy. The system, as embodied in the WTO, mediates international trade relations such that trade can take place in a stable and predictable, rules-based environment with instruments for the settlement of disputes. The system has benefited WTO member economies by delivering improved access to export markets and helping members to defend their market access rights. It has also promoted the sustained development of sound economic policy by providing guarantees against policy reversal and by making promises of future reforms credible. The WTO system is particularly important to non-OECD countries for at least two reasons. First, it constrains OECD countries that have enough bargaining power to unilaterally influence the behaviour of others. Second, the system contributes to a healthy, growing world economy which developing nations need in order to maximise growth.

While globalisation provides substantial economic opportunity, the ability to seize this opportunity and address any negative impacts depends on an appropriate policy framework. Experience points to certain key elements that tend to be included in successful approaches: macroeconomic stability, adequate labour supply and human capital, appropriate social protection and respect for core labour standards, sound environmental practice and good governance (*e.g.* with respect to regulation, corruption, effective policy development processes, conflict resolution), among others. Adopting complementary policies to reinforce social cohesion appears to be particularly important in sustaining the drive towards trade liberalisation. In the poorest countries, development co-operation can play a role by fostering capacity building to ensure that institutions are able to implement the requisite policies.

The advance of trade liberalisation

Great strides have been made in opening the world economy to trade. Since the Second World War, eight rounds of multilateral trade negotiations succeeded in lowering the average (trade-weighted) most-favoured-nation tariff rates on industrial goods from roughly 40 % to around 4 %. In addition to broad-based tariff reductions, the most recent rounds of trade negotiations have resulted in the easing of some important non-tariff barriers, thereby enhancing the prospects for further trade expansion. It has been estimated that once the Uruguay Round agreements are fully implemented, the share of imports from non-OECD countries affected by OECD countries' non-tariff barriers (including the Multi-Fiber Arrangement-related restrictions) will drop from around 18% to roughly 5%. Along with progress on the traditional agenda of tariffs and non-tariff barriers, the Uruguay Round delivered progress in other areas. The result was the signing of three new agreements (the General Agreement on Trade in Services, the Agreement on Trade-Related Aspects of Intellectual Property Rights and the Agreement on the Application of Sanitary and Phytosanitary Measures) and the reform of the Agreement on Technical Barriers to Trade.

Trade liberalisation resulted, at first, in better integration primarily for the OECD countries. However, during the last two decades, a number of new players have entered the stage. These non-OECD countries have taken deliberate steps to open their economies wider to the outside world through a combination of unilateral, regional and multilateral liberalisation initiatives. With rapid growth, these countries see their stakes growing in a well-functioning world economy and are preparing themselves to engage substantively in the discussion of how and when to open markets further and to deepen and broaden international rule-making or understandings that affect trade.

In order to help put the impact of economic openness in perspective, it is instructive to consider estimates of the net results of trade liberalisation under the Uruguay Round compared with what would have been obtained in its absence. Taking into account dynamic effects, these estimates reveal a net increase in world income of roughly 1 to 2 % of Gross Domestic Product (GDP). While different models using different assumptions and liberalisation scenarios can lead to different results, the estimates nevertheless illustrate the substantial global benefit from just one round of trade liberalisation. While the largest welfare gains in *absolute* terms have tended to accrue to OECD countries, many non-OECD countries have gained more relative to their GDPs.

The globalisation of production, facilitated by trade liberalisation, is yielding additional benefits to non-OECD countries. It has created domestic opportunities for developing countries to absorb new and more efficient processes, over and above the direct benefits from expanding export-related trade, output and employment growth. The spillover effects of production sharing processes include the diffusion and absorption of new and improved production technologies, management and labour skills, and of information about world markets. In turn, these lead and facilitate the upgrading of quality, the introduction of new products and catching-up with best practices in the world economy.

Enhancing the multilateral trading system

Developing nations have increasingly focused on a several priorities for the multilateral trading system including expanding market access for products and services, improving rules and disciplines, enhancing provisions for special and differential treatment and increasing the scale and effectiveness of technical assistance. There is a crosscutting goal of a timely and complete implementation of all Uruguay Round Agreements. Specific issues concern enhancements in the system with respect to both existing and contemplated measures.

Market access

Market access represents perhaps the single most important trading issue between OECD and non-OECD countries. Many developing countries continue to face barriers to market access that limit their ability to reap the full potential benefits of trade. Agricultural producers encounter high tariffs, quotas and subsidies that constrain their export potential. Multi-Fiber Arrangement-related quotas on textiles and clothing are set to be phased out by 2005, but many of these products will remain subject to relatively high tariffs. Some sensitive industrial products are subject to escalating tariffs that also limit export prospects. Market access has also been hindered by contingency protection measures and indeterminate measures (*e.g.* voluntary export restraints). Balanced development of merchandise trade links between OECD and non-OECD countries requires progress in reducing remaining trade restrictions, especially on product categories where non-OECD countries enjoy a comparative advantage such as certain labour-intensive manufactures and agricultural products.

There is also a tremendous potential for expansion of international trade in services. The service sector is already the fastest growing component of both trade and foreign direct investment. The agreement to create a General Agreement on Trade in Services (GATS) was one of the major innovations to emerge from the Uruguay Round and a contributing factor to the growth in the sector. GATS offers the benefits of the multilateral trading system such as the stability and civility available under the rules and the binding of commitments on market access and national treatment (which WTO member countries assume in their national schedules). However, to harness the full potential of the GATS, countries will need to use the opportunity of the current negotiations (under the built-in agenda from the Uruguay Round) to aim for a significant expansion in the number and coverage of commitments.

For developing countries, one of the largest potential areas for commercially meaningful tradeoffs concerns liberalisation of mode 4 services trade, involving the temporary entry of service providers. Although traditionally a sensitive policy area in many OECD countries, labour mobility is one issue where incremental progress could be made in the new GATS round. It is also an area where opposition within OECD countries is not monolithic - there are indeed many "user" industries that would benefit from - and clamour loudly for - more liberal temporary access regimes, and the development of coalitions with such industries could help change the *status quo*.

The service sector is an area where trade liberalisation can have favourable influences on the domestic economy more broadly. Services are essential inputs into the production of virtually all other goods and services, and producers depend on services to deliver their output to end-users. Expanded trade opportunities in this area can increase the range and quality of services that are available, with major effects on overall economic performance.

Rules

Among the most important accomplishments of the Uruguay Round for non-OECD countries was the strengthening of the rules governing the conduct of international trade, their extension to new areas of activities, and the assurance of protection through an enhanced dispute settlement procedure. Under the WTO, there are systems for surveying the operation of these disciplines and discussing problems or issues that may arise (*e.g.* the Council for Trade in Goods, the Council for Trade-Related Intellectual Property Rights and the Anti-Dumping Committee). Areas governed by such disciplines include, for example, trade-related investment measures (TRIMs), trade-related intellectual property rights (TRIPS), the use of anti-dumping and countervailing measures and customs valuation procedures.

The strengthening of dispute settlement procedures in the WTO, in particular, greatly enhanced the credibility and integrity of multilateral trade disciplines and provided a more reliable mechanism for dispute resolution. In effect, the Uruguay Round Agreements constituted a rule-writing exercise intended to forestall the protectionist abuse of other types of government interventions (especially domestic policies), while establishing a level playing field for national policies and increasing their predictability. At the same time, some developing nations have expressed particular concern with the existing rules (*e.g.* anti-dumping, countervailing duties, safeguards, and technical barriers to trade) and contemplated rules (*e.g.* in respect of trade and environment). In some cases, there are concerns expressed about excessively burdensome implementation problems and inadequacy of provisions to safeguard the interests of "developing countries".

Implementation issues are often cited with respect to TRIMS and TRIPS agreements. For example, some non-OECD countries have cited the TRIMs Agreement as having an inadequate transitional period for phasing out such investment measures and have called for extension of compliance deadlines. This concerns, for example, local content requirements in the automotive sector. Moreover, several non-OECD countries have argued that intellectual property protection under the TRIPs Agreement is largely oriented towards areas of interest to developed countries, leaving aside areas that particularly interest other countries, like indigenous knowledge or geographical indications for traditional handicrafts. Moreover, some countries point out that compliance with the TRIPS Agreement is particularly difficult for "developing countries," given that most of them had to start work on IPRs from scratch and lacked the necessary human resources and expertise.

Many non-OECD countries have also expressed concerns about the number of anti-dumping measures taken against their products. (However, it is interesting to note that between 1995 and 1999, non-OECD countries have filed a total of 632 anti-dumping cases against 595 filed by OECD countries). Some non-OECD countries are particularly concerned that anti-dumping measures may increase substantially in the textiles and clothing sector once the MFA-related quantitative restrictions are phased out. These countries have called for a prohibition of repeated anti-dumping investigations on the same product within a year, as well as for making it mandatory rather than "desirable" to impose a smaller margin of anti-dumping duty when this would suffice to remove injury from domestic industry. Anti-dumping procedures are resource-intensive and, as such, they tend to weigh more heavily on small-sized economies than on others. Moreover, for countries whose exports are concentrated in relatively few sectors, anti-dumping duties may have a disproportionate impact on their economies.

Special and differential treatment

The majority of non-OECD countries benefit from some degree of preferential access to many OECD markets. More than two-thirds of the WTO's roughly 140 members are considered to be developing countries. Despite extensive references in the WTO agreements to special provisions, rights and obligations for developing countries, there is no official definition of what constitutes a "developing country." GATT Contracting Parties have self-elected their designation, most recently when the WTO was created. In all, there are some 145 special and differential treatment provisions operating within the WTO system. These include (1) provisions aimed at increasing developing countries' trade opportunities; (2) provisions that call upon WTO members to safeguard the interest of developing countries; (3) flexibility of commitments; (4) transitional time periods; and (5) technical assistance. They are spread across various accords such as the Multilateral Agreements on Trade in Goods, GATS, TRIPS, the Understanding on Rules and Procedures governing the Settlement of Disputes, and various Ministerial Decisions.

A number of developing countries have expressed dissatisfaction with the actual operation of many of special and differential treatment provisions. They consider these to be inadequate instruments to help them integrate more fully into the multilateral trading system. On the other hand, developed countries increasingly take the view that no single system can address the interests and concerns of a diverse group of countries, such as the developing nations. Already, the Uruguay Round agreements incorporated a limited application of the concept of tiering of some benefits across different groups of developing countries. That is, in some cases more generous treatment was accorded to least developed countries, countries with a per capita income less than $1 000[1] (known as Annex VII countries), and net food importing countries.

There remains pressure for further differentiation. Critics point out, for example, that even where problems and their magnitudes are roughly similar across countries, the remedies appropriate to a country like Singapore (with per capita income of $26 600 in 1998) are probably different from those appropriate to Ghana (with a per capita income of $400 in 1998). In rare cases where the remedies are the same, it nevertheless remains likely that the capacity of Singapore to adopt them is different from that of Ghana. Further differentiation in the treatment of "developing countries" might be accomplished in a number of ways. One approach would continue and extend the practice initiated during the Uruguay Round of targeting more benefits to a select group of developing countries. An alternative approach would involve graduation of the more advanced developing countries from the group, either on a self-initiated basis or by using analytical criteria based on economic indicators. Whichever approach might eventually be selected, it is clear that multilateral co-operation in this area is of critical importance. At the same time, ensuring that the WTO works more effectively to the benefit of all its members is a responsibility for all nations to share.

Capacity building

In order to benefit more fully from the multilateral trading system and better integrate into the globalising world economy, some developing countries are pursuing a comprehensive development strategy aiming to facilitate private sector-driven development. This entails continued efforts at liberalising trade and investment regimes, building supply-side capacities, and enhancing the competitiveness of the private sector, among other actions. It is by no means an easy task and, in the trade area, will require major efforts to help these countries strengthen their basic human and institutional capacities.

The objective of enhanced international integration has been incorporated in goals articulated by development community and embodied in the Comprehensive Development Framework. International institutions, donors and host-countries are translating this framework into action through country-specific poverty reduction strategies where trade reforms play a central role. In addition, capacity-building and technical assistance programmes are being specifically designed to assist the less advanced developing countries with their integration efforts.

Conclusions

Openness offers the potential for creation and preservation of value and wealth, and a much more reliable way to develop constructive responses to challenges than bureaucratic centralism. Over fifty years ago, the major economic powers realised that reducing barriers to the international flows of goods and services was vital to economic recovery from the Great Depression and the Second World War, as well as to future growth. This realisation was pursued over succeeding decades in a process of trade liberalisation leading to the establishment of the WTO in 1995 with provisions to support additional liberalisation in the future.

For developing nations, trade has served as a primary means for achieving integration into the global economy. The multilateral trading system has addressed key interests of these non-OECD countries, but many consider that they have not seen the full potential benefits of existing arrangements and that additional work is needed. Market access still represents perhaps the single most important trade issue between OECD and non-OECD countries, but there are many others. At the same time, a distinction can be made between those issues already embodied in existing WTO agreements, those which require new rules, and those which are not within the scope of the multilateral trading system as defined by the WTO members. Effective resolution of the full range of issues will require that each be considered in the appropriate international forum, with due regard to coherence across international institutions.

A multilateral round represents the best chance to address the multiple trade-related issues in a process yielding mutual benefits. This is because it offers a wide range of potential tradeoffs and a broad scope for gain due to the coverage of a large number of markets. The WTO's consensus approach is oriented toward guiding the process toward win-win solutions, meaning that the WTO membership as a whole must be satisfied that the results are balanced. Consequently, undertaking a multilateral round is a tremendous task but well worth the global effort by OECD and non-OECD countries alike.

Note

1. Unless otherwise indicated, currency amounts in this report refer to US dollars.

INTRODUCTION

Trade liberalisation continues to be an important issue (for all countries and irrespective of their level of development) both practically – because there is still a long way to go in dismantling trade barriers – and intellectually – as controversy continues to fuel the debate on its role in economic development. There are undoubtedly other equally important policies for development – *e.g.* education, health, infrastructure and macroeconomic management – but a bad trade policy is likely to reduce their beneficial effects, even possibly to the point of rendering them ineffective. A very restrictive trade policy probably permits other policies to get further out of line, and if trade policy is arbitrary and interventionist it affects the whole government/business relationship.

This study examines the intellectual and the practical issues arising in the context of multilateral trade liberalisation efforts, focusing exclusively on the experiences in non-OECD countries (*i.e.* the developing countries and transition countries). The study intends to contribute to a clearer understanding of the interests, needs and concerns of non-OECD countries in the multilateral trading system. Towards that objective, two separate, though not mutually exclusive building blocks are set up. The first addresses the role of trade and trade policies in economic development, while the second examines the contribution (actual and potential) of the WTO to the goal of sustainable development.

The fuller integration of non-OECD economies in the world economy ranks among the top priorities for OECD countries. The fundamental objective is to ensure that non-OECD countries share in the creation of, and benefit from, global economic growth. One key element of this approach is to maintain and indeed strengthen wherever possible, a free and open, rules-based multilateral trading system for the benefit of all participants and their societies.

The year 1995 ushered in a new era of multilateral economic co-operation with the creation of the WTO, the only international body dealing with rules of trade between nations. The WTO established the legal basis for the new multilateral trading system as a single, indivisible undertaking, where membership is conditional on countries having schedules of concessions and commitments on market access in industrial and agricultural products, as well as commitments on intellectual property rights and in the services sector. This concept of a single undertaking underlying the WTO brought an end to the fragmentation of the multilateral trading system in different layers of obligations and rights, while simultaneously responding to increased demands for stronger enforcement of international trading rules.

While the Uruguay Round Agreements in effect did no more than respond to emerging trends in the globalising world economy, this "re-tooling" of the multilateral trading system has implied, *inter alia*, a change in perception among its members regarding the costs and benefits of trade rules, be they current and/or in the making. This is an unsurprising development when set against the recent record of integration of non-OECD economies. Countries that have embraced the forces of globalisation by liberalising and reforming their economies were the ones that have reaped the most benefits from buoyant world markets; those that have not saw their fortunes stagnate and in some instances decline.

Despite the long-term benefits of the Uruguay Round Agreements, a number of non-OECD countries are referring to difficulties in implementing some of them and, in some cases, an inability to make full use of WTO disciplines. In addition, they are expressing concerns over the lack of effective market access in areas of export interest to them; they are questioning the adequacy of the provisions for special and differential treatment (S&D) and technical assistance to help them with their integration efforts.

Non-OECD countries include economies at various stages of development. Within this broad group, the least developed countries (LDCs) are often given special consideration as the weakest partners in the international community. They face important structural problems, often compounded by natural or human-invoked disasters. In order to take full advantage of the potential benefits of the multilateral trading system, they will need to develop their human and economic capital and overcome difficulties in implementing some of the Uruguay Round Agreements. However, even within this group, significant differences are still evident: the trade performance of African LDCs has been particularly weak in contrast to the relatively stronger performance of Asian exporters like Bangladesh, Cambodia and Laos.

One could also distinguish among other countries in the non-OECD area on the basis of various economic and social indicators, such as different thresholds of per capita incomes, the extent of participation in world trade, and others. The study argues that such distinctions provide a fruitful basis for an informed discussion on the various aspects of special and differential treatment.

Notwithstanding the differences in economic performance among the non-OECD countries, the Uruguay Round introduced provisions that impart greater flexibility and special and differential treatment that are in principle accessible to countries self-defined as developing in the context of the WTO. Additional provisions were also granted to LDCs (known as Annex VII countries and defined as those with a per capita income less than $1 000), and to net food importing developing countries. Subsequent to the Uruguay Round, other initiatives, including the Integrated Framework for Trade-Related Technical Assistance for LDCs, have been introduced with the objective of supporting the trade-related aspects of these countries' development and poverty reduction strategies.

The study is organised in seven Chapters. Chapter I begins by describing the challenges facing policymakers in a globalising world economy. Chapter II then illustrates the current global trends in trade and investment flows and the extent of non-OECD countries' participation. Chapter III reviews and assesses the contribution of open trade and investment regimes to economic growth in non-OECD countries. Four main conclusions are drawn:

1. The global trends in trade and investment, while very positive, have not benefited all countries equally.
2. Despite the econometric difficulties of establishing beyond doubt that openness enhances growth, the weight of the evidence is quite clearly in that direction. Certainly, there is no coherent body of evidence that it is bad for growth.
3. Trade liberalisation is a *sine qua non* of the overall reform process
4. ,A country reform plan designed to enhance its integration into the global economy and sustain a drive towards trade liberalisation will require complementary policies that re-enforce social cohesion by minimising adjustment costs. This includes, *inter alia*, providing hard and soft infrastructure and establishing conflict resolution schemes and social safety nets.

With these conclusions in mind, Chapters IV and V then examine the actual and potential contribution of the WTO to the goal of sustainable development in non-OECD countries. This second building block of the study rests on four pillars: (1) market access for goods and services, (2) rules and disciplines , (3) special and differential treatment and (4) development co-operation.

In Chapter IV, attention is focused on how the multilateral trading system, as embodied in the WTO, can yield benefits for non-OECD countries. The analysis focuses on two main aspects. The first addresses the particular benefits non-OECD countries derive from the multilateral trading system. The second reviews the achievements of the Uruguay Round in the area of trade in goods and services, and illustrates where future liberalisation efforts could serve to allay non-OECD countries' concerns in this area. Despite major progress in dismantling tariff and non-tariff barriers to trade through eight rounds of multilateral trade negotiations, market access still represents perhaps the single most important trading issue between OECD and non-OECD countries. Non-OECD countries' strongest demands are not only for continued access to OECD countries' markets, but also for increased access. On the other hand, OECD countries look for non-OECD governments to participate more effectively in multilateral negotiations, and for some of them to contribute more to liberalisation and rule-making efforts and to assume more WTO obligations. In other words, some non-OECD countries should "graduate" from the WTO status of "developing country" that confers special and differential treatment under the rules, and preferential access to OECD markets.

Issues related to special and differential treatment are taken up in Chapter V which identifies the potential role of the WTO in helping non-OECD countries sustain their drive towards global integration and reaping the most benefits. The concerns voiced by non-OECD countries with five different sets of provisions under special and differential treatment are distinguished and discussed. These are provisions concerning non-OECD countries that: (1) aim at enhancing their trade opportunities ; (2) call on WTO members to safeguard their interests; (3) grant them flexibility in the implementation of certain rules and disciplines; (4) allow them transitional time periods; and (5), extend technical assistance.

Chapter V also provides four different approaches to targeting or "tiering" various benefits across different groups of countries in the WTO. These may prove useful in the context of discussions on "graduation" of certain WTO members from the status of "developing country." The approaches are based on different sets of economic variables using different time periods. The focus is on a group of non-OECD, non-least developed countries WTO members whose per capita income does not exceed $9 300 in 1998. Countries with a per capita income larger than $9 300 have been excluded from the analysis since they belong to the category of "high income" countries as defined by the World Bank. The options presented here are meant as an illustration of how the issue might be tackled.

While per capita incomes define the level of economic development for any one country, they need to be supplemented by other economic variables that are directly related to trade performance given the mandate of the WTO. The most obvious supplemental indicators in the study are: the share of country *i*'s trade in its gross domestic product; the share of country *i*'s trade in the trade of WTO members; the total number of commodities exported by country *i*; the terms of trade of country *i*; and the share of the net value of a country's food import bill in its total merchandise imports and/or exports. The first two variables are taken to reflect the degree of a country's participation in international trade, while the last three can be thought of as measures of a country's degree of vulnerability (or lack thereof).

Chapter VI examines the implications of development co-operation for trade drawing on work being currently undertaken by the Development Assistance Committee of the OECD (DAC). The Chapter sets out the strategies and programmes of the donor community that aim to assist non-OECD countries in their efforts to enhance their integration into the global economy. The fundamental objective is to ensure that their people are able to share in the benefits generated by the globalisation process. And, finally, Chapter VII presents some concluding remarks.

I. THE TRADE AND INVESTMENT ENVIRONMENT GOING INTO THE 21ST CENTURY

The establishment of the WTO in 1995 was probably the boldest initiative in multilateral economic co-operation in half a century. It represented the culmination of a collective effort by representatives of more than 120 economies to establish firmer international norms for the conduct of international trade in both goods and services. The WTO established the legal basis for the new multilateral trading system as a single, indivisible undertaking, where membership is conditional on countries having schedules of concessions and commitments on market access in industrial and agricultural products, as well as commitments on intellectual property rights and in the services sector. Membership in the WTO also implies acceptance of the General Agreement on Tariffs and Trade (GATT) 1994 (which includes GATT 1947 and all amendments and protocols to it) as well as all of the Uruguay Round Agreements. This concept of a single undertaking underlying the WTO brought to an end the fragmentation of the multilateral trading system in different layers of obligations and rights, while simultaneously responding to the need for stronger enforcement of international trading rules.

While the decades following World War II were characterised principally by closer integration among OECD countries, in the last two decades new players have entered the stage. A rapidly expanding group of non-OECD countries have taken deliberate steps to open their economies wider to the outside world through a combination of unilateral, regional and multilateral liberalisation initiatives. This is reflected in an average increase in their trade to GDP ratios of 4% a year during the period 1981-98, while their ratios of foreign direct investment (FDI) to GDP rose by an average annual rate of 17% (Figure 1.1). With rapid growth, these countries see their stakes growing in a well-functioning world economy and are hence preparing themselves to engage substantively in the discussion of how and when to open markets further and to deepen and broaden international rule-making or understandings that affect trade.

Figure 1.1. Trends in openness to trade and FDI in non-OECD countries, 1980-98

The trade and FDI-led integration process depicted in Figure 1.1 above has accelerated markedly beginning in 1991. During the 1980s, reform efforts were mainly concentrated on removing barriers to trade at the border and to a more limited extent, barriers to capital flows. More recently, as the process of trade liberalisation took hold, pressures of international competition have led more and more non-OECD countries to focus their reform efforts on domestic, market-oriented policies and practices. International norms, rules and disciplines have often played a critical and decisive role in shaping these countries' reform agendas. China, for example, has defined its trade reform programme with a view towards membership in the WTO, and the same objective has underlined its commitments on intellectual property rights. Similarly, the agreements between the Russian government and the IMF also contain explicit commitments by Russia to abide by WTO principles in anticipation of its eventual membership.

It is true that the trend towards trade and investment liberalisation has proceeded at different speeds at different times, but the fact remains that the trend is world-wide. More and more non-OECD countries are liberalising imports, promoting exports, encouraging foreign investment, and decontrolling foreign exchange regimes. Such a strategy has already propelled a number of them into the front ranks of trading nations and recipients of foreign investments.

The unprecedented growth in cross border flows of goods, services and investment has fundamentally altered the landscape of the world economy. In virtually every dimension of economic life we are experiencing ever-increasing levels of international economic activity, both in absolute terms and relative to the level of national activity. This is the phenomenon economists refer to as globalisation, which represents the forging of closer production and distribution links across different markets.

In addition to the world-wide trend towards liberalisation, globalisation has also been driven by technological advances that have shortened the economic distance among nations. Technological innovations, especially in information and communication technology have contributed to a decline in transaction costs for individual firms, allowing them to pursue world-wide sourcing strategies with the consequence of a widening in the range of enterprises for which global operations are commercially viable. Competition between global firms is increasingly being conducted in the area of new technologies and production processes. Moreover, new technologies, along with regulatory innovations, have made it possible to supply many infrastructure services on a competitive basis and have opened up possibilities for international trade in such services. At the same time, research and development costs and the economies of scale involved are fostering new strategic alliances between firms.

With the dispersal of production and of marketing processes world-wide, the competitiveness of firms has been enhanced by greater efficiency in the use of factors of production and in the design of customised products in close contact with end-users. Simultaneously, globalisation has entailed a blurring of the identity of firms and of products. This has presented new challenges to governments in managing their economies and contributed to a growing sense of economic uncertainty among economic actors as they face strong international competition and the need for adjustment. All these factors are undermining the traditional separation between the domains of domestic and international policies.

Importantly, as the process of globalisation continues to reduce the economic distance among countries and regions, as well as among the economic actors themselves, the pressure on policy interaction in traditional areas of multilateral co-operation is intensifying. The most obvious manifestations of this have involved governments in continuing efforts to remove tariff and non-tariff barriers to trade, and to extend the coverage of liberalisation efforts in such areas as government procurement and agriculture.

In addition, closer economic integration among nation states has "internationalised" a range of policy domains that previously were either simply neglected, or considered an exclusively national preserve, or else were subject only to comity like co-ordination and consultation arrangements. As a result, major multilateral initiatives have led to negotiations, and in some instances agreements, in new areas such as trade in services, the protection of intellectual property rights, and investment. Other issues, such as competition policy, international labour standards, environmental policies, company law, immigration policies, monetary matters including debt and development, political stability and alleviation of poverty have been proposed by some governments during the Marrakech meeting in April 1994 (at the conclusion of the Uruguay Round) as matters ripe for international negotiation.

More generally, governments have demonstrated increasing concerns with a broad range of policy-related determinants of competitiveness. The globalisation of economic activity has nurtured a growing interest in the numerous ways in which the conditions of market access may be influenced. Perhaps the area where this concern is most noticeable is in standard-setting and domestic regulation more generally. Sensitivity to the notion that regulations can be manipulated to tilt the conditions of competition in favour of a subset of economic actors, together with the perception that sharply divergent preferences in such matters as environmental quality and social policy are increasingly crucial determinants of competitive advantage, have added to pressures for harmonisation in many policy areas. Such harmonisation may be negotiated, or may come about through *de facto* competition among regulatory systems. Whichever approach dominates, the imperative felt by governments to ensure that their economic constituencies are not placed at a disadvantage through sharply different approaches to policy intervention can be a source of significant friction at the international level.

Policymaking is also confronted with other challenges as the economic performance of countries has diverged. As will be seen in Chapter III, countries that were able to align themselves with the forces of globalisation and embrace the reforms needed to do so (*e.g.* by liberalising markets) were the ones that have gained the most from buoyant international trade and capital flows. Others have seen their fortunes stagnate, and in some instances decline.

As the WTO Ministerial Conference in Seattle and the subsequent IMF/World Bank meetings in Washington and in Prague showed, concerns have been voiced and actively pursued by civil society regarding the agenda of trade liberalisation and its potential impact on poverty reduction, income distribution and environmental sustainability. In the WTO context specifically, some non-OECD countries are questioning the current priorities and progress, and are wary of linkages between trade policy and broader issues such as labour standards and the environment. They are expressing concerns over lack of effective market access in areas of export interest to them; they are making reference to difficulties in implementing some Uruguay Round Agreements, and, in some cases, to an inability to make full use of WTO disciplines. Managing this friction is one of today's most pressing challenges for policy-makers.

II. THE GLOBALISATION PROCESS AND NON-OECD COUNTRIES

Globalisation is a multi-faceted process that describes economic and social forces that have produced rapid growth in world trade, even faster integration of the world's financial markets, and the spread of international production networks. One important consequence of these developments is that economies of vastly different levels of development are being drawn together through more extensive trade and investment flows. This is the growth dynamic of globalisation which implies ever-increasing economic feedback from non-OECD to OECD countries and vice versa, strengthening the links between these countries and enhancing the prospects for economic growth. While trade and investment linkages between OECD economies remain predominant, the ties that bind countries at different stages of development are closer today than ever before.

As will be discussed below, there is a close connection between the emerging patterns of global FDI, those of world trade and those of international production networks. The internationalisation of production stimulates trade flows between investment home and host countries as cross-investments between countries proliferate. While intra-OECD trade still accounts for almost three-fourths of world trade and intra-OECD foreign investment for roughly 65% of total OECD outward FDI, these shares are declining and should continue to drop as barriers to trade and investment fall in non-OECD countries. Trade and investment flows have also grown dramatically among non-OECD countries over the last decade. However, a few non-OECD countries have succeeded in joining the dynamism underlying trends in investment, global production sharing activities and international trade.

A. Investment

Cross-border capital flows began to experience spectacular growth in the mid-1980s. The liberalisation and deregulation of financial markets, privatisation of state enterprises, advent of new information technologies and emergence of new financial instruments have combined to create an environment conducive to growth in cross-border capital flows. For example, the value of cross-border assets held by banks more than tripled between 1973 and 1998; average daily turnover in foreign exchange markets has grown from about $200 billion in the mid-1980s to more than $1.4 trillion today; this is equivalent to approximately 87% of all countries' foreign exchange reserves. Even after allowing for resale, daily foreign exchange transactions amount to well over $700 billion, more than 50 times the value of total world-wide trade in merchandise and services. In addition, cross-border transactions in bonds and equities in the major advanced OECD economies reached more than 100% of GDP in 1998, as compared to 10% just ten years ago.

Foreign direct investment has grown at close to 17% per annum during the period from 1981to 1998, more than twice as fast as world-wide trade in goods and services and nearly five times faster than GDP(Panel A, Table 2.1). Global outflows of FDI experienced more than a ten-fold rise - from $59 billion in 1981 to $617 billion in 1998.

Most dramatic has been the more than 16-fold increase between 1981 and 1998 in FDI flows to non-OECD countries, from $10 billions to $160 billions (Panel B, Table 2.1). FDI inflows have become the dominant form of resource flows to non-OECD countries, and their benefits go well beyond finance. These include technology transfer, the development of human capital and the promotion of foreign trade.

Private portfolio flows to non-OECD countries have also grown dramatically since 1981 as pension funds and other institutional investors in OECD countries have sought greater portfolio diversification through investment in overseas markets, including non-OECD markets. On the demand side, low international interest rates and improved creditworthiness have spurred new international bond issues as well as an upturn in foreign bank borrowing. In 1997, total borrowing on international markets reached $1.4 trillion, of which $105 billion or 8% was undertaken by non-OECD economies, up from less than 5 percent just a decade ago. However, the financial crisis that beset some economies in 1997 has significantly reduced non-OECD countries' access to the international capital markets. Net long-term flows to non-OECD countries in 1998 declined to $261 billion, down from their record level of $328 billions in 1997 (Table 2.2).

The data reported in Table 2.2 describe the trend towards a more prominent role for private flows and the relative decline of official development finance. The share of private flows in the total has doubled between 1990 and 1998 and it now accounts for almost 82% of total net flows to non-OECD economies. Since 1993, FDI-related net capital inflows to non-OECD economies are larger than official development finance and their share in total in 1998 stood at 65%. Debt financing contributed some 27% of net capital inflows while portfolio equity investments made up close to 6%. As such, portfolio equity flows constitute a standard form of investment into non-OECD economies.

Despite these overall positive developments, wide disparities have emerged across non-OECD countries. Table 2.3 shows that a group of only 23 countries accounted for 90% of the total $141 billion in FDI flows to non-OECD countries in 1998, In fact, two non-OECD countries (China and Brazil) were the destinations of more than half of the FDI flows into the non-OECD area.

B. The Globalisation of production

Another important development in the last two decades has been the increasing role played by multi-national enterprises (MNEs) and their networks of affiliates in world markets. In 1980, the share of foreign assets in world GDP was 18% (Table 2.4); during the period 1980-1995, the accumulation of foreign assets dramatically accelerated, reaching 57% of world GDP in 1995. This is more than 3 times the level at the beginning of the Century. The value-added output of MNE affiliates (that is, excluding the output of parent firms in their home countries) as a share of world GDP in 1995 has been estimated at 7.5%, up from 4.5 in 1975. In the non-OECD area, that share had reached 6.3% in 1995, up from an estimated 4.4% in 1982.

Recent studies (Yeats 1997 and World Bank 1997) suggest that overseas production by MNE affiliates is becoming increasingly oriented towards exports rather than the domestic market of the host country. The combination of lower trade barriers and liberalisation more generally, and falling transportation and communication costs have stimulated and facilitated firms' efforts to increase their efficiency by re-organising their production processes globally according to the comparative cost advantages of different locations. These efforts, in turn, have led to important structural shifts in the patterns of global production and of international trade.

Up until the late 1960s, the globalisation of manufacturing activities involved mainly the production of primary commodities in non-OECD countries for export to the OECD area for further processing. Beginning in the early 1970s, these activities began to be re-oriented towards the production of specialised, labour-intensive goods with relatively higher value-added than primary commodities. Thus, major parts of production processes within vertically integrated international manufacturing industries have been re-located across the globe to capitalise on the comparative cost advantages of different locations.

For example, firms in the OECD area buy plastic toys from Hong-Kong, China that were produced in mainland China based on raw materials imported from Malaysia. Integrated chips are fabricated and etched in the US, assembled in Mexico and re-exported to the US for final sale. The search for cost advantage also extends to individual segments of the production process. For example, the production of a particular car by one major US auto maker draws on inputs originating from nine different countries: 7.7% of the cost of the car goes to Germany for design, 17.5 to Japan for components and advanced technology, 30% to Korea for assembly, 4% to Chinese Taipei and Singapore for minor parts, 2.5% to the UK for advertising and marketing, and 1.5% to Ireland and Barbados for data processing. This means that only 37% of the production cost of an "American" car is actually generated in the US.[1] The globalisation of production activities means more specialisation between nations in different branches of manufacturing, and even within different stages of production.[2]

The significance of the "slicing-up" of the production processes can be seen from the growing importance of trade in parts and components in the machinery and transport sector. This trend reflects both the export of these goods to low cost assembly or processing locations, and their import from low cost production locations. In 1995, OECD countries' exports of parts and components (in the machinery and transport sector) amounted to $442 billion, 5 times their levels in 1978 (Table 2.5). Data limitations preclude a detailed examination of non-OECD countries' exports of parts and components, although available estimates suggest that countries such as Singapore, Chinese Taipei, and Malaysia all had exports in excess of $10 billion each (World Bank, 1997).

The lower panel in Table 2.5 identifies the fastest growing non-OECD destinations for OECD countries' exports of parts and components. These totalled $67 billion in 1995 eight times their level in 1978 or 15% of all OECD component exports. In 1995, China was the single largest non-OECD destination after experiencing the most dramatic increase of 55-fold between 1978 and 1995. Thailand and Malaysia saw their shares increase by a factor of 18 during the same period, while Indonesia's share rose by a factor of 10. However, and as has been the case with FDI, few non-OECD countries have become tied up with the global economy through production sharing activities.

The benefits to non-OECD countries from the globalisation of production are potentially large, especially when considering how such activities enhance the domestic opportunities to absorb new and more efficient processes, over and above the direct benefits from faster trade, output and employment growth that such activities promote. The spillover effects of production sharing processes include the diffusion and absorption of new and improved production technologies, management and labour skills, and of information about world markets. In turn, these lead and facilitate the up-grading of quality, the introduction of new products and catching-up with best practices in the world economy. In short, global production sharing could potentially have significant positive spillover effects on productivity growth by strengthening know-how and skills of both firms and labour. Equally telling is how it can potentially promote and facilitate the integration of countries into the world economy.

C. International trade

(i) Merchandise trade

Measured by the volume of merchandise exports alone, the world economy has become increasingly integrated in the years since the Second World War. The volume of world merchandise trade is today about 18 times what it was in 1950, a period during which the value of world output increased by a factor of 6 (Figure 2.1). The period since 1950 saw more than a doubling, from 7 to 14%, of the ratio of world exports to global production.

Figure 2.1. **Trends in World Merchandise Exports and GDP, 1950-1998 Volume Indices, 1990=100**

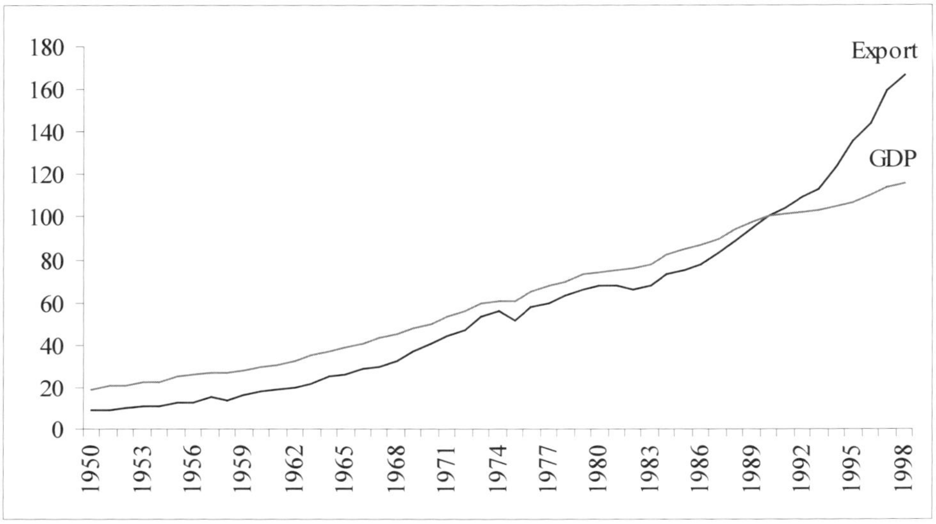

The accelerating pace of trade-led integration has been remarkable: during the period 1985-98, the ratio of trade to world GDP rose three times faster than in the preceding decade, and nearly twice as fast as in the 1960's. An important feature underlying this trend over the past two decades has been the heightened involvement of non-OECD countries. During the period 1987-97, merchandise trade of non-OECD countries grew at an annual rate of 11%; this is more than twice the rate of growth of their GDPs during the same period (5.3% excluding countries in Eastern Europe and in the Commonwealth of Independent States). This compares with 8 and 11% growth rates, respectively in OECD and in world merchandise trade (Table 2.6). Consequently, non-OECD countries' share in world trade rose from less than 17% in 1987 to 24% in 1997. Trade among non-OECD countries is also on the rise: in 1997, they sold more than 26% of their exports to each other, compared with less than 20% a decade ago.

In recent years, the economies of OECD and non-OECD countries have become more closely intertwined than they have ever been. OECD countries now depend on non-OECD countries for a third of their exports sales (as compared with less than 18% two decades ago), a fifth of their primary commodity imports, and almost half of their petroleum consumption. For their part, non-OECD countries rely on OECD countries for more than 60% of their trade and 47% of their primary commodity imports.

Not only did non-OECD countries deepen their involvement in world trade, many have also managed to diversify their trade linkages. During the period 1950-75, the share of manufactured products in non-OECD countries' total exports was relatively low and stagnant (hovering between 40 and 45%). Beginning in the late 1970s, this share began to increase. tracing an upward sloping line that continued its climb unabated throughout the last two decades to reach 83% in 1997.

In 1985, a typical non-OECD country exported no more than 79 products for which the export value exceeded $50 000 (Table 2.7). By 1990, the number of products with export value greater than $100 000 had risen to 114, and in 1995 to 128 products. During the same period, the concentration index (ranging between 0 and 1 with one being maximum concentration) declined from 0.47 to 0.36. The share of trade in GDP in these countries stood at 44% in 1997, more than twice its level in the 1980s. These trends reflect the industrialisation process that many non-OECD countries have been undergoing; they also point to the increasing role of international trade in their domestic economic activities.

Trade-led integration has proceeded relatively rapidlyfor countries in East Asia and some in Latin America,non-OECD Europe and Central Asia; elsewhere this process has proceeded slowly (Table 2.6). During the period 1987-97, annual growth in merchandise exports of Sub-Saharan Africa (SSA) averaged 5.6%, exactly half the rate that underlined the growth of non-OECD countries' exports (11.2%). Thus, SSA's share in world trade fell from 4% in 1987 to 1.3% in 1997. Countries in the Middle East and North Africa experienced even lower growth rates than SSA's and thus ended the period with a share in global merchandise trade of 2.3%, down from 7% in 1987. South Asia also experienced a more than halving of its share in world merchandise exports: from 2.6% in 1987 to 1.1% in 1997.

(ii) Trade in services

International trade has also been experiencing important structural shifts. Rapid advances in information and communication technology are expanding the boundaries of tradability in services - the fastest growing component of both trade and FDI. Many international transactions, which previously would have been considered prohibitively expensive, have now become commonplace because of the ease with which people can move and communicate electronically across national boundaries.

Services, which include activities as diverse as the transportation of goods and people, financial intermediation, communications, distribution, accountancy, hotels and restaurants, education, health care, and construction, account for a substantial and rising share of output in every economy. Even in the lowest-income countries, services account for more than a third of GDP. In middle-income countries, services generally account for more than 50% of output and an equal if not greater share of employment.[3]

For the better part of the last decade and a half, services have also been the fastest growing component of cross-border trade and investment activity. Estimates show that total measurable trade in services, as defined by the various "modes of supply" subject to multilateral disciplines under the WTO's General Agreement on Trade in Services (GATS), stood at some $2.2 trillion in 1997 (Table 2.8).[4] This represented 7.6% of world output and over a third of total trade in goods and services.

Although OECD countries dominate global trade and investment in services, non-OECD countries are the most specialised in - and dependent on - services exports as a source of foreign exchange earnings. In most instances, this reflects the importance of tourism and transportation-related activities. But a growing number of non-OECD countries are also becoming large exporters of transactions processing, back office services and a burgeoning range of information and software development services. The potential to exploit recent and emerging technological developments that allow cross-border trade in services and provide firms with incentives to slice up the value chain geographically is enormous.

(iii) Services, the new economy and development

Today's interconnected economy is influencing more than productivity growth. It is making knowledge a more important factor of production than labour, raw materials or even capital. Just as important, it offers the potential of levelling the playing field, by shaping a more equitable relationship between OECD and non-OECD economies. Four broad characteristics of the emerging borderless service economy help to illustrate such a seemingly counter-intuitive proposition:

- The first is the increasing indifference of the new economic landscape to geography, distance and time. Transaction costs for consumers and businesses alike will fall rapidly as many steps that intervene between buyers and sellers – distribution, sales, retailing – are compressed. By far the most significant impact of the development of electronic commerce will be the falling barriers and costs to market entry. Starting a new business and contesting new markets will be much easier, allowing a far greater number of suppliers to enter markets. Small and medium-sized enterprises, alongside large multinational corporations, can now be full participants in the global marketplace. Businesses in non-OECD countries can now overcome many of the obstacles of infrastructure, capital and transportation, which limited their economic potential in the past. At the end of the day, consumers all around the world will be the main beneficiaries of such growing competition.

- Second, service industries, especially finance and telecommunications, are creating the reality of a global infrastructure for the world economy. This infrastructure is greatly facilitating the adjustment and redeployment of old industries and the development of new ones. It also holds the key to allowing non-OECD countries to narrow the gap that separates them from the OECD world.

- Third, the global services economy is essentially a knowledge-based economy, with information and ideas as its most precious resources. Unlike the classical factors of production – land, labour and capital – information and knowledge are not bound to any region or country but are highly mobile and almost infinitely capable of expansion. This knowledge-based economy is not so much replacing other economic activities – software is not about to substitute for the food we harvest and eat or the cars we manufacture and drive. But it is fundamentally altering the nature, timeliness and quality with which goods are produced, brought to market or traded across borders.

- These changes lead to a fourth characteristic, namely the borderless economy's potential to equalise relations between countries and regions. This is so because of its capacity to open the way to free and equal access to information and knowledge. While the gap between the richest and poorest is still unacceptably wide, the economic and technological means to address the digital and other divides are already in place. The last few years have seen many non-OECD countries leap-frog phases of industrial and technological development – for example in mobile telephony, with far-reaching implications for the efficiency of activities as diverse as small-scale farming, health care delivery or inventory management.

It should come as little surprise, then, that many non-OECD countries have in recent years undertaken far-reaching regulatory reforms targeted at increasing the contestability of domestic service sectors (see Box 2.1). To a significant extent these reforms have been driven by changes in technologies that have facilitated the provision of services at much lower cost and allowed competition to emerge in markets that were traditionally regarded as natural monopolies. Service sector reforms have also been pushed by manufacturing and agricultural interests, as well as by upstream service "users," who have come to be subject to greater international competition as merchandise trade and regulatory barriers were lowered. In order to benefit from the process of globalisation and its attendant "splintering" or "fragmentation" of the production chain, enterprises must have access to efficient service inputs. As nations have reduced tariffs and other barriers to trade, effective rates of protection for manufacturing industries may become negative if they continue to be confronted with input prices that are higher than they would be if services markets were contestable.

Box 2.1. The economy-wide importance of service sector efficiency

The importance of policy in the service sector goes beyond the sector itself. Services are essential inputs into the production of virtually all other goods and services, and producers depend on services to deliver their output to end users. Because the price and quality of the services available in an economy have major impacts on all sectors, service sector policies typically exert major effects on overall economic performance.

Services play an increasingly important role in the economy of all nations. Products are becoming increasingly time sensitive, both because of shorter product life-cycles and because of the pervasive use of 'just-in-time' production management techniques. Foreign buyers must be assured that a supplier can deliver to specification and on time. For suppliers in non-OECD countries to be competitive, they must be able to rely on efficient service industries that can provide inputs that are tailored to their needs. Restrictions on services trade and investment lead to lower quality and/or higher cost service inputs. As a result, liberalisation can bring large efficiency and welfare gains.[5]

Recent efforts to quantify existing barriers surveyed in François and Hoekman (1999) suggest that competition-inhibiting barriers tend to be relatively low in business services, consulting and distribution services compared to barriers in transportation, finance, and telecommunications. The latter are basic "backbone" services that are crucial to the ability of enterprises to compete internationally. With the exception of transportation, policies towards these sectors appear to be significantly more restrictive in non-OECD countries.[6]

A number of country-specific exercises have been undertaken that demonstrate the economy-wide implications of policy reform in services. Hoekman and Konan (1999) for instance used a computable general equilibrium (CGE) model of Egypt to assess the orders of magnitude that may be involved in eliminating service sector inefficiencies. Their work showed that as a result of services trade liberalisation, the potential welfare gains to Egypt could be as high as 13%. If in addition Egypt were to reach a mutual recognition agreement with the EU, the potential welfare gain accruing to Egypt could reach 20%. They also noted that the greater the extent to which regulatory and administrative practices give rise to resource costs (frictional or transactions costs), the greater the welfare improvement that would result from reform. Chadha (1999a) used a multi-country CGE model that separated out India, and ran simulations making different assumptions regarding prevailing market structures in agriculture, manufacturing and services. He concluded that Indian welfare would expand by between 0.7 to 1.4% of GDP following a 25% global reduction in the assumed vector of services protection. His work also showed that other countries in South and Southeast Asia could expect efficiency gains of up to 3% of GDP.

Such results are quite large relative to what is usually found using similar types of models to assess the impact of merchandise trade liberalisation. They are strongly indicative of the potentially great gains to be reaped from regulatory reform and greater competition in service industries. Many policy-makers have long known this intuitively-, fuelling a strong push towards unilateral trade and investment regime liberalisation in services.

D. Trade, investment and disparities

So far, we have described how trade and investment lead the way to market integration. However, it is obvious that the rising tide of trade and investment did not lift all boats equally. There have been wide disparities among non-OECD countries across all the trends described above, notwithstanding the substantial overall growth.

What factors explain these divergent trade performances, where some countries have been more dynamic than others in taking advantage of emerging global trade opportunities? Part of the answer has already been given. Rapid growth in trade depends on constructing not only strong trade links with other countries, but equally importantly strong investment links that encourage the absorption of new production and managerial techniques, and improve international competitiveness. The globalisation of production structures takes place through investment abroad, which in turn stimulates trade. It is thus unsurprising to find that the same non-OECD countries that were able to attract the bulk of FDI were the ones that participated most vigorously in production sharing arrangements, and which experienced the most dramatic increases in their shares in world trade (Table 2.9).

Attracting FDI and participating in international specialisation through trade depends crucially on implementing the right policy framework. The next Chapter will examine the defining elements of this framework. At this point, suffice it to state that countries that have been able to align their economies with the forces of globalisation and embraced the reforms needed to do so by liberalising markets were the ones that have gained the most from buoyant international trade and capital flows. These economies were able to create competitive industries, stimulate domestic and foreign investment, exploit economies of scale, and facilitate technology transfer and the adoption of best-practices techniques.

However, the success stories achieved through outward-orientation involved more than the opening of markets and a welcoming environment for international investment. Policies for macroeconomic stability, good governance, etc. are also of crucial significance. So too, for example, are the right environmental policies to ensure that development is sustainable. The feasibility and durability of trade reforms, and the extent to which they and other policy reforms contribute to growth will also depend critically on the speed of adjustment. That, in turn, is closely linked to conditions in labour markets and the speed with which private investment responds to new opportunities. Political leadership is also crucial when it comes to managing many of the difficult social issues that accompany the liberalisation process.

One reason that some non-OECD countries have resisted the movement towards a more liberal trade regime is concern over short-term costs associated with structural adjustment. Adjustment is associated with change, and change can be disruptive. Import-competing industries in the economy that were operating behind protective walls and government intervention may not be able to sustain capacity utilisation, employment and hence output following liberalisation. Both workers and entrepreneurs engaged in these industries may face hardships as returns to their physical and human capital are altered. Some may also suffer as a result of the dissipation in rents that accrued to them when they operated behind protective walls.

While these private costs are temporary, they are of course offset by higher and permanent returns to other workers and entrepreneurs, especially those engaged in export sectors. These redistributions of income may play an important part in defining the political feasibility and sustainability of trade reforms. In this respect, it must be emphasised that protection has never been proven to be an efficient means of sustaining employment. Careful examination of the factors affecting employment shows that protection actually "costs" better paying jobs otherwise created by the export sector. Jobs saved in industries protected are often offset by viable jobs forgone elsewhere in the economy. On its own, protection is a poor alternative to positive adjustment policies. This will be even more so in a globalising world economy. A country that attempts to cut itself off from the stream of world development forgoes the advantages of dynamism abroad: this is a sure way of locking itself into relative decline.

E. The Social dimension of globalisation: core labour standards

There is a correlation between the level of economic development and adherence to core labour standards. This has been confirmed in a recent OECD study, "International Trade and Core Labour Standards," showing that in respect of freedom of association, the most economically developed countries enjoy above-average standards, while many of the poorest countries generally do not comply. This is a two-way process. As has been pointed out through the ILO Working Party on the Social Dimension of Globalisation, gains from the globalisation of trade and investment can be discerned in terms of higher economic growth, which in turn is associated with adherence to core labour standards. At the same time, strengthened core labour standards themselves can contribute to economic growth and efficiency (see Box 2.2). While economic growth is a prerequisite for social progress, growth in itself is not enough to guarantee that progress. Growth must be accompanied by certain social ground rules that enable all those involved to share in the wealth they have helped generate.

Core labour standards are accorded particular importance internationally because they reflect basic human rights in the workplace, provide for framework conditions that facilitate the meaningful application of other labour standards and promote the expression of free choice that is a key element in the healthy functioning of market economies. The ILO Declaration on Fundamental Principles and Rights at Work, adopted in 1998, embodies these principles and rights which include freedom of association and the effective recognition of the right to collective bargaining; the elimination of all forms of forced or compulsory labour; the effective abolition of child labour; and the elimination of discrimination in respect of employment and occupation. This Declaration obligates all member countries to respect the core labour standards and includes a two-step follow-up procedure to promote compliance.

In the 1996 WTO Singapore Declaration, trade ministers renewed their commitment to internationally recognised core labour standards, recalled that the ILO was the competent body to set and deal with these standards, reaffirmed support for the work of the ILO in promoting these standards and rejected their use for protectionist purposes (see Appendix 1 for background). Formal recognition of the corresponding ILO conventions has also increased; since October 1995, the number of countries that have ratified the seven original fundamental ILO conventions has more than doubled. However, follow-up is still required to improve monitoring and to engage non-ratifying countries. And - although there has been some improvement - there remain substantial gaps between the ratification of the fundamental conventions and the application of principles in practice.

Development co-operation, in fostering growth, will have a major role to play in helping bridge these gaps, particularly with respect to child labour and related issues. In addition to enforcement of national legislation based on recognised minimum standards, effective solutions to the problem of child labour have required action in such areas as poverty eradication, improving the situation of women, increasing access to, and the quality of education, and the provision of social security.

Box 2.2. The economic properties of core labour standards

The OECD publication *International Trade and Core Labour Standards,* draws two broad conclusions from recent literature.

1. Strengthened core labour standards can increase economic growth and efficiency.
2. Countries with low core labour standards do not enjoy better export performance than high-standard countries.

Stiglitz (2000), in challenging the neo-classical assumption that labour is just another factor of production, argues that the "high road" to economic development (which he takes to include the right to collective bargaining) can increase economic efficiency by, *inter alia,* promoting the increased buy-in by workers to the goals of the immediate work group. He also argues that collective bargaining can enhance the overall efficiency of the economy by facilitating income redistribution that would not occur, or would be more costly to implement, through the tax/welfare system. Stiglitz also cautions, however, that this is a delicate balance and that excessively strong unions can, through collective action, interfere with the efficiency of the economy.

ILO (1998) also addresses the economic benefits that can result from the enforcement of core labour standards. It concludes that child labour is detrimental to development since it means that the next generation of workers will be less well educated; collective bargaining and tripartite dialogue are necessary elements for creating an environment that encourages innovation, higher productivity, and foreign direct investment inflows; and, the discrimination faced by women and minority groups are important obstacles to economic efficiency and social development.

Palley (1999) refers to evidence in an OECD 1996 study that, on average, countries which improved rights of freedom of association experienced an increase in GDP growth and manufacturing output in the five-year period afterwards (OECD, 1996b, pp. 87,131).[7] He extends this analysis by controlling for the effects of earlier growth in the countries concerned and for the impact of growth elsewhere. For the countries examined, he concludes that improved freedom of association increased growth by between 1.2 and 1.4 percentage points on average.

Adherence to core labour standards can also affect a country's ability to withstand external shocks. A recent study (Rodrik, 1996) considers the impact of adverse shocks that affected developing countries during the 1970s. The results of that analysis suggest that countries that develop democratic institutions - which here are taken to include core labour rights - before the transition to trade liberalisation will weather the transition with smaller adverse consequences than countries without such institutions.

Recent studies suggesting a negative relationship between observance of labour standards and trade performance do not challenge the finding of the 1996 OECD study that countries with low core labour standards do not enjoy better export performance than high-standard countries because these recent studies focus on labour standards generally and not on *core labour standards.* This distinction is crucial for analytical purposes because core and non-core labour standards are expected to have different, and often opposite, effects on economic outcomes. Standards such as working time and minimum wages can affect patterns of comparative advantages, *e.g.* higher minimum wages are likely to affect trade performance negatively. But core labour standards, unlike minimum wages, will not necessarily affect comparative advantage negatively and may indeed have a positive effect.

The question of trade sanctions to promote adherence to core labour standards remains highly controversial - particularly among developing countries. In the case of child labour, for example, some recent literature suggests that governments of countries in which children are employed may choose to change their laws and/or improve their enforcement rather than bear the cost of trade sanctions. It is also suggested that, in certain circumstances, a ban on child labour may be effective in shifting the economy into an equilibrium where adult wages are high and children do not need to work. This could apply to countries with relatively high labour productivity that are able to support all their children without sending any to work. However, the literature also suggests that, in very poor countries, a ban may worsen the condition of households. Moreover, a ban on the import of goods which have used child labour as an input might drive child labour out of export industries but is likely to do little to prevent child labour in the informal sector which is the major employer of child workers in such countries.[8]

Recent analysis, drawing on experience in Brazil and Mexico, suggests that a subsidy to families to keep their children in school is likely to be a superior policy to, for example, trade interventions, in terms of curbing child labour. It is well recognised that trade interventions are not an optimal instrument to abolish exploitative child labour and expand human capital formation. Nor would trade sanctions sit well with the finding that countries with low core labour standards do not enjoy better export performance than high-standard countries (see Box 2.2 above). However, it should also be recognised that so long as there is a failure to take actions that are optimal, some will seek to keep trade sanctions in the mix of policies under debate.

This said, there are many examples of trade, or trade-related, policies and practices being used in order to create incentives for adherence to core labour standards. These include private-sector codes of conduct, labelling schemes and unilateral action under the Generalised System of Preferences. A primary objective of the US GSP scheme, for example, is to encourage the promotion of improved workers' rights in beneficiary countries. According to the ICFTU, the threat of withdrawal of US GSP brought changes to the labour code and improved rights to collective bargaining and freedom of association for workers in a number of countries of Central America and the Caribbean, most notably in the Dominican Republic.

A recent development within OECD also bears on efforts to promote core labour standards. In June 2000, a comprehensive review of the OECD Guidelines for Multinational Enterprises was completed. One chapter of the Guidelines addresses employment and industrial relations. It urges firms to: respect workers' rights to freedom of association; to provide information and facilities to employee representatives; to communicate effectively with employees so as to enable them to obtain a fair view of the enterprise's performance; to train employees; not to engage in discrimination in their employment practices. The review resulted in inclusion of recommendations in relation to those core labour standards that were not specifically covered in the original guidelines (child labour and forced labour, in particular). In addition, other sections of the Guidelines deal with issues that are relevant to labour standards. For example, they recommend that companies encourage application of the Guidelines within their supply chain.

Other organisations and mechanisms also seek to promote labour standards. As noted in the OECD studyon *International Trade and Core Labour Standards*, there are a number of private sector codes of conduct, regional agreements, and unilateral government actions that provide incentives for the promotion and implementation of core labour standards. In addition, the international financial institutions increasingly recognise and promote core labour standards through their policies and programmes.

While economic development is a key factor associated with improved application of core labour standards, it appears that there is a growing consensus that various unilateral, multilateral, and private mechanisms can also contribute to the promotion and support of these standards. ILO initiatives constitute the central element in the global approach to dealing with core labour standards issues. This foundation is complemented and supported by a range of development assistance programmes beyond the ILO that seek to contribute to addressing the problem of compliance at the source, as well as by guidelines, codes and unilateral incentive-based schemes designed to promote compliance. To paraphrase the 1996 OECD Trade, Employment and Labour Standards study, because of the multifaceted nature of the problem, various mechanisms can potentially address at least one reason for non-observance of core labour standards. However, none can solve all the problems at the same time.

F. The Environmental dimension of globalisation

The environmental implications of globalisation can be both positive and negative, depending on the pace and direction of economic growth and the robustness of the environmental policy frameworks established in each country. As OECD Ministers pointed out in 1995, in general terms, trade liberalisation will have a positive impact on the environment by improving the efficient allocation of resources, promoting economic growth and increasing general welfare, provided effective environmental policies are implemented.[9] But in the absence of effective environmental policies, including those aiming at internalising environmental costs, or when distortive domestic policies exist, increased economic activity generated from trade liberalisation can contribute to environmental problems.

Designing and implementing effective environmental policies remains a challenge in most countries and particularly in non-OECD countries (Box 2.3). Building capacity here is an important activity of donor programmes in partnership with beneficiaries. At the same time, trade liberalisation also has an important link with environmental protection through the identification of so-called "win-win" solutions where greater market access can also promote environmental and development benefits. Recently both the WTO and OECD have undertaken work on trying to highlight how the removal of trade restrictions and distortions in certain sectors can promote environmental benefits. There exist "win-win" solutions in which a better allocation of economic resources lessens the demands made by production on the environment and render social benefits.

Subsidies with environmentally harmful effects are certainly a major cause for perpetuating the vicious circle that characterises the slow development of non-OECD countries. Through the effects of distorting international prices, subsidies encourage overproduction and, as a consequence, overexploitation of national resources. Furthermore, subsidisation impedes non-OECD countries from exporting their goods since overproduction in rich countries dumped on the international markets depress prices, making non-OECD countries' products uncompetitive. To remain in the market, low cost producers are forced to sell at lower prices at the expense of their environment and delaying their development.

"Win-win" solutions can be pursued by implementing reforms that line up trade liberalisation, environmental protection and development objectives. According to a sectoral analysis issued by the WTO Committee on Trade and Environment, if adverse production and consumption externalities are adequately internalised into decision-making processes, trade and environmental objectives can become mutually supportive.[10] Studies in sectors such as environmental goods and services, agriculture, fisheries, and fossil fuels, and others, show the positive relationship between the removal of trade restrictions and the improvement of the environment. A more efficient allocation of factors, enhanced competition, a reduction of poverty, a sustainable rate of natural resources exploitation and, also, an increased availability of environmental-related goods and services through market liberalisation are among the positive effects to be expected.

Box 2.3. Assessment methodologies: tools to identify environmental impacts of trade liberalisation

Reconciling trade and environmental policies to ensure they are mutually supportive is not an obvious task. Countries need to adopt an integrated, cross-sectoral and comprehensive approach to guiding the implementation of sustainable development. Among other tools, environmental assessments (also called environmental reviews) represent analytical instruments aimed at helping trade negotiators, in both OECD and non-OECD countries, to predict probable environmental impacts of liberalisation measures.

Many developed countries (the United States, Canada, Norway and the EU) have committed to undertake reviews of future trade liberalisation in order to identify those measures more likely to exacerbate environmental pressures. These examples of environmental assessment generally follow the way paved by the 1994 OECD Methodologies on environmental and trade reviews. At that time, the OECD was a precursor in indicating the importance of assessing environmental effects of trade liberalisation agreements.

More recently, UNEP has also been playing a crucial role in developing a comprehensive methodological approach to environmental reviews: The Reference Manual for Integrating Assessment of Trade-Related Policies ("the Manual").[11] In line with non-OECD countries' requests, UNEP is supporting investigations carried out by research institutes in non-OECD countries on how trade impacts not only on the economy, but also on the environment and development. The Manual provides a general and neutral approach for integrated (economic, environmental and social) assessment so that policy-makers in non-OECD countries can ensure that policies ensure that trade and other economic liberalisation policies foster sustainable development.

In addition to investigating negative and positive effects of trade liberalisation, UNEP capacity building plays a fundamental role. For this purpose, UNEP works closely with governments to assist them in their efforts to enhance their institutional and human capacities for integrating environmental considerations into development planning.

In a similar vein, UNEP and UNCTAD are co-operating in the field of trade, environment and development to further strengthen country capabilities to promote economic expansion in an environmentally friendly way. The UNEP-UNCTAD Capacity Building Task Force on Trade, Environment and Development (CBTF), launched in March 2000, represents the result of this common effort.[12] The major aim of the CBTF is that of combining the strengths of these two organisations in their respective realms to strengthen the capacities of non-OECD countries in pursuing sustainable development. One of the main objectives of this project is to enhance capacity building through the promotion of country studies, training, policy dialogue and information exchange.

(i) Environmental goods and services

Liberalising trade in environmental goods and services can, for many reasons, be assumed *prima facie* to bring together the elements of a 'win-win' situation. In opening domestic markets to the international economy by reducing tariffs and other trade-distorting measures, advanced know-how and environmental technologies will become more readily available: trade in services and capital goods is the most direct channel for transfer of technology. Reducing tariffs and other trade-restricting measures means that services and goods will be cheaper. Limited environmental protection budgets can be stretched further. Trade liberalisation also provides incentives for the generation of technological progress through expansion of market opportunities.

More indirectly, opportunities to realise economies of scale and effects of increased competition on efficiency can be expected to lead to welfare gains. Subjecting firms to international demand patterns gives firms incentives to undertake investment in environmental technology. Finally, liberalisation of world goods and services markets can provide the necessary pre-conditions for technology co-operation in order to generate innovations more closely associated with domestic economic and environmental conditions. In other words, this can help increase local capabilities for domestic technology innovation and adaptation, relative to dependence on transfer of foreign technology.

Research carried out on the liberalisation of water and waste management services markets in non-OECD economies indicate increased foreign participation in the provision of water and waste management services where such sectors are liberalised.[13] Overall, a number of "win-win" outcomes for non-OECD countries from trade and investment liberalisation (*i.e.* foreign participation) in the provision of water and waste management services was found:

Environmental benefits that may be secured from increased trade in these environmental services include:

- First and foremost, the roll-out of clean water and waste collection services to much greater numbers of citizens, leading to healthier human environments;
- Reductions in the wastage of and/or inequitable access to scarce water resources (*e.g.* through leaks and ease of bypass/siphoning associated with old/inadequate pipe infrastructure);
- Increased availability of drinking water from the introduction of recycling of effluent water for industrial use (which also, once established, produces cost-savings for industry);
- Use of waste recycling to create alternative sources of energy (*e.g.* gas and electricity from garbage recycling systems for use by households, light industry, power stations, fertilisers for small farms);
- In-country presence of foreign firms creates increased opportunities for environmental management education and training, and skills transfer, to other commercial sectors, both for the water and waste media and other environmental services;
- Availability of a larger choice of environmental technologies addressing the environmental problems more appropriately for the country in question which can often mean a move away from end-of-pipe solutions to preventive ones.
- Reinvestment of a share of profits in research and development of new environmental technologies and skills, environmental infrastructure upgrades and new environmental investments.

Economic efficiency and development benefits that may be secured from increased trade in these environmental services include:

- Relief of pressure on government budgets, including at state and municipal level. Savings may be reallocated to environmental policy, inspection and enforcement budgets, to other social services and to the overall budget balance.

- Creation of skilled and unskilled jobs for local workers, in design, construction and long-term operation of the facilities;

- Availability of water and waste management systems attracts foreign and local investment to the community, bringing more jobs, stable economic growth and an increased local tax base;
- Local private sector partners extend their experience in big and/or very specialised projects which can be (and are being) exported to other countries with similar needs and operating conditions;
- Build-operate-transfer operations revert to local ownership at a specified time, and comprise significant environmental resources, and sources of jobs, into the future;

Trade "wins" include:

- Local and foreign companies participating in this trade gain new opportunities to deploy their skills and technologies;
- At a global level, trade and investment liberalisation will improve resource allocation through the application of comparative advantage.

(ii) Agriculture

A reduction of barriers to *agricultural* trade will influence the overall scale of agricultural activities, the structure of agricultural production in different countries, and the mix of inputs and outputs. These adjustments will likely have both positive and negative impacts on the environment. Preliminary results from work in the OECD Joint Working Party on Agriculture and Environment suggest that trade liberalisation will lead to a reduction of agricultural prices and production intensity in countries that have had historically high levels of fertiliser and pesticide application, so that environmental stress in these countries would be relieved. Countries where increases in production intensity occur might be able to accommodate increased application rates of agro-chemicals relatively easily, as their historical levels of fertiliser and pesticide use tend to be low. Hence, agricultural trade liberalisation is expected to lead to an overall reduction in the risk of water pollution associated with the use of agro-chemicals. Yet, the impact of a reduction in barriers to agricultural trade on other environmental effects, such as soil erosion and biodiversity, and the provision of perceived benefits from agriculture in terms of landscape appearance is difficult to evaluate in general, as these effects and benefits tend to be highly site-specific. In order to avoid a potential increase in soil erosion and biodiversity reduction, or a loss of landscape benefits, targeted environmental policy measures might need to be implemented.

(iii) Fisheries

The fisheries sector is characterised by too many vessels and fishers chasing too few fish. Species with a high market value are likely to be fully exploited. If fished out, the fishing capacity (vessels and equipment) moves on to their next target. This is possible in the fisheries sector due to the ease with which fishing fleets can re-flag and as such change nationality.

In addition to traditional gains from freer trade, market liberalisation in the fisheries sector may, concurrently, bring environmental and other economic, tangible and non-tangible benefits. While the effect of transfers on resource sustainability is difficult to determine, as there are many influences on fish stock health that are difficult to disentangle, capacity-reducing subsidies can reduce pressure on fish stocks, when combined with appropriate management measures. In the meantime it is important to recognise that all measures taken in the fisheries sector (trade policy measures included) will take effect against the background of the management system in place. Attempts to further liberalise fisheries markets should be made without causing adverse impacts on resource sustainability. It is useful to consider the fact that some trade measures are implemented by regional fisheries management bodies, *e.g.* trade restrictions for Atlantic Bluefin Tuna by ICCAT, in order to help achieve effective fisheries management and resource conservation.

Whilst tariffs are at a fairly low level in most OECD member countries (or reduced further through tariff preferences), it remains the case that, during the last decade, a number of other potential barriers to trade have been put in place. These concern in particular the use of sanitary and technical requirements to trade in fish and fish products. Many of these requirements are expensive to put in place and may as such be a significant burden for some non-OECD countries.

Table 2.1. **Trends in GDP, FDI and trade, 1981-1998**

A - World

Year	GDP	FDI	Trade
1981	17434	59	3902
1982	17533	42	3638
1983	17973	40	3584
1984	18846	50	3791
1985	19454	53	3838
1986	20108	82	4211
1987	21022	131	4975
1988	21967	152	5739
1989	22746	188	6546
1990	23322	192	7512
1991	25881	146	8522
1992	26331	158	9567
1993	26682	206	9270
1994	27471	231	10274
1995	28213	311	12104
1996	29199	347	12674
1997	30245	439	13035
1998	30705	617	12802
Average growth (%) 1981-98	3.3	16.7	6.9

B - Non-OECD countries

Year	GDP	FDI	Trade
1981	2923	10	705
1982	2966	10	666
1983	3037	9	640
1984	3278	8	630
1985	3348	10	642
1986	3534	9	634
1987	3891	11	731
1988	4061	16	819
1989	4176	25	1196
1990	4260	21	1338
1991	4354	29	1294
1992	4428	40	1798
1993	4577	57	1679
1994	4755	74	1819
1995	4964	95	2116
1996	5148	114	2251
1997	5377	153	2389
1998	5392	160	2267
Average growth (%) 1981-1998	3.4	21.1	7.9

Source: World Bank, *World Development Indicators*

Table 2.2. **Net resource flows to non-OECD countries, 1990-98 ($ billions)**

	1990	1991	1992	1993	1994	1995	1996	1997	1998
Total flows	97.0	118.0	145.8	209.9	208.8	244.8	295.9	327.8	261.3
Official flows	56.9	62.6	54.0	53.3	45.5	53.4	32.2	39.1	47.9
Private flows	40.1	55.4	91.8	156.6	163.3	191.4	263.7	288.7	213.4
of which									
Private debt flows (*)	15.7	18.6	38.1	49.0	54.4	60.0	100.3	105.3	58.0
Portfolio equity flows	3.7	7.6	14.1	51.0	35.2	36.1	49.2	30.2	14.1
Foreign direct investment	20.7	29.2	39.6	56.6	73.7	95.3	114.2	153.2	141.3

(*) Private debt flows include: commercial banks loans, bonds and other private flows.

Source: OECD, Development Assistance Committee

Table 2.3. **Main beneficiaries of FDI inflows to non-OECD Countries, 1998**

Country	FDI (millions US $), 1998	Share in total non-OECD FDI, 1998
China	43 751	31.0
Brazil	31 913	22.6
Thailand	6 941	4.9
Argentina	6 150	4.4
Malaysia	5 000	3.5
Chile	4 638	3.3
Venezuela	4 435	3.1
Colombia	3 038	2.2
Russia	2 764	2.0
India	2 635	1.9
Romania	2 031	1.4
Peru	1 930	1.4
Philippines	1 713	1.2
Panama	1 206	0.9
Vietnam	1 200	0.8
Kazakhstan	1 158	0.8
Egypt, Arab Rep.	1 076	0.8
Nigeria	1 051	0.7
Azerbaijan	1 023	0.7
Lithuania	926	0.7
Croatia	873	0.6
Bolivia	872	0.6
Ecuador	831	0.6
All above	127 155	90
Remaining non-OECD countries	14 135	10
All non-OECD countries	141 290	100

Source: World Bank, *World Development Indicators*

Table 2.4. **Multinational enterprises in the global economy**

Share of foreign assets in world GDP (%)	
1870	6.9
1900	18.6
1914	17.5
1930	8.4
1945	4.9
1960	6.4
1980	17.7
1995	56.8

Share of MNE output in		
	World GDP	Non-OECD GDP
1970	4.5	
1977	5.4	
1982	5.8	4.4
1988	6.3	
1990	6.4	3.9
1992	6.2	4.3
1995	7.5	6.3

Table 2.5. **Destinations of OECD countries' exports of parts and components**

Destinations	1978		1995	
	Value ($ million)	Share (%)	Value ($ million)	Share (%)
World	84 418	100.00	441 531	100.00
OECD	54 327	64.35	298 829	67.68
Non-OECD	30 091	35.65	142 701	32.32
By main non-OECD country destination				
China	193	0.23	10 668	2.42
Singapore	863	1.02	9 736	2.21
Hong Kong, China	554	0.66	8 554	1.94
Taiwan	927	1.10	7 734	1.75
Thailand	396	0.47	7 197	1.63
Malaysia	325	0.38	5 917	1.34
Brazil	1 399	1.66	5 150	1.17
Indonesia	464	0.55	4 618	1.05
South Africa	1 351	1.60	4 007	0.91
Saudi Arabia	1 893	2.24	3 038	0.69
All Above Destinations	8 365	9.91	66 618	15.09
All Others	21 726	25.74	76 083	17.23

Source: Ng and Yeats (1999)

Table 2.6. **Growth of current merchandise trade, by direction, 1987-1997**

Source of exports	High-income importers							Low- and middle-income importers								
	US	EU	Japan	Other OECD	All OECD	Other high-income	All high-income	Sub-Saharan Africa	East Asia and Pacific	South Asia	Europe and Central Asia	Middle East and North Africa	Latin America and the Caribbean	All low- and middle income	World	Share in world trade 1997
High-income countries	**9.5**	**6.8**	**5.3**	**10.4**	**7.5**	**9.8**	**7.7**	**5.2**	**15.8**	**11.6**	**10.1**	**6.1**	**11.5**	**11.3**	**8.4**	**75.8**
- OECD	9.0	6.5	3.6	10.2	7.1	8.0	7.2	4.6	15.6	10.7	9.7	4.9	11.5	10.5	7.8	64.9
- United States	...	5.9	3.4	9.2	6.3	6.6	6.4	7.2	18.5	13.0	12.0	4.2	13.9	13.5	8.1	15.5
- EU-15	8.4	5.8	4.5	12.3	6.6	10.0	6.7	3.8	16.3	11.0	9.6	3.6	6.3	8.3	7.0	34.8
- Japan	8.8	9.1	...	5.3	8.1	8.5	8.2	1.6	12.7	3.9	3.4	8.4	7.0	10.1	8.9	5.5
- Other OECD	9.5	11.1	2.2	12.1	9.9	9.0	9.8	3.8	16.4	9.9	12.6	10.8	12.3	12.3	10.0	9.1
- Other high-income	12.2	12.3	9.6	12.2	11.3	17.3	12.5	16.5	16.1	16.2	16.5	11.7	13.7	15.4	13.3	10.9
Low / middle-income countries	**13.1**	**9.6**	**9.3**	**8.0**	**10.3**	**17.5**	**11.5**	**12.1**	**15.2**	**9.6**	**7.4**	**7.5**	**13.6**	**10.4**	**11.2**	**24.2**
- Sub-Saharan Africa	7.0	2.6	-1.9	6.5	2.8	9.7	3.7	12.4	10.6	15.2	1.6	19.2	7.9	11.6	5.6	1.3
- East Asia and Pacific	16.4	13.9	14.3	11.5	14.3	20.3	16.5	13.7	21.3	20.0	9.5	27.0	15.1	18.7	16.9	8.7
- South Asia	7.7	4.7	0.3	9.1	4.8	12.8	7.0	23.9	4.6	12.4	-1.0	10.6	9.9	8.1	7.3	1.1
- Europe and Central Asia	9.9	13.4	1.7	6.9	12.3	19.5	12.6	5.3	7.8	-0.2	8.6	1.2	3.9	7.4	10.4	6.2
- Middle East and North Africa	6.9	4.7	0.9	4.3	4.6	7.0	4.9	13.0	7.5	6.6	-6.0	5.7	7.3	4.2	4.7	2.3
- Latin America and Caribbean	14.4	9.7	9.5	6.5	12.0	18.2	12.4	10.1	26.9	33.0	11.3	-1.4	15.8	14.5	12.9	5.6
World	**10.5**	**7.2**	**6.2**	**10.1**	**8.0**	**11.9**	**8.5**	**6.8**	**15.7**	**11.1**	**8.9**	**6.5**	**12.1**	**11.0**	**9.0**	**100.0**

Note: Growth rates are compound averages
Source: IMF, Direction of Trade Statistics

Table 2.7. **Export concentration & diversification indices for selected non-OECD economies**

	1985			1990			1995		
Country or area	Number of commodities exported[1]	Diversification index	Concentration index	Number of commodities exported[2]	Diversification index	Concentration index	Number of commodities exported[3]	Diversification index	Concentration index
Argentina	151	0.685	0.184	214	0.65	0.142	221	0.564	0.125
Bahrain	55	0.892	0.802	99	0.889	0.829	108	0.865	0.629
Barbados	31	0.88	0.622	82	0.748	0.292	66	0.759	0.199
Belize	13	0.933	0.419	34	0.875	0.402	15	0.952	0.572
Bolivia	24	0.939	0.584	51	0.906	0.321	102	0.797	0.215
Brazil	163	0.528	0.122	210	0.529	0.101	220	0.517	0.088
Brunei Darussalam	7	0.854	0.677	54	0.864	0.599	63	0.883	0.517
Cameroon	47	0.752	0.403	103	0.796	0.311	84	0.848	0.323
Chile	100	0.848	0.341	183	0.809	0.396	199	0.794	0.313
Colombia	115	0.756	0.489	172	0.71	0.296	210	0.631	0.223
Congo	25	0.818	0.894	34	0.879	0.797	41	0.882	0.557
Costa Rica	100	0.769	0.352	129	0.718	0.281	154	0.718	0.303
Côte d'Ivoire	120	0.796	0.372	106	0.878	0.345	121	0.905	0.408
Cuba	71	0.893	0.733	9	0.969	0.863	86	0.9	0.461
Cyprus	106	0.658	0.197	91	0.773	0.21	97	0.749	0.228
Dominica	12	0.919	0.598	17	0.951	0.649	51	0.769	0.426
Dominican Republic	65	0.862	0.43	6	0.977	0.454	85	0.793	0.209
Ecuador	47	0.79	0.616	77	0.845	0.486	156	0.808	0.373
Egypt	83	0.765	0.541	163	0.661	0.225	152	0.737	0.244
El Salvador	76	0.789	0.557	97	0.745	0.415	131	0.72	0.35

(continued, next page)

Table 2.7. **Export concentration & diversification indices for selected non-OECD economies (con't)**

	1985			1990			1995		
Country or area	Number of commodities exported[1]	Diversification index	Concentration index	Number of commodities exported[2]	Diversification index	Concentration index	Number of commodities exported[3]	Diversification index	Concentration index
Fiji	37	0.891	0.683	59	0.845	0.352	74	0.845	0.32
Gabon	28	0.824	0.79	45	0.893	0.812	36	0.931	0.73
Ghana	33	0.882	0.544	54	0.907	0.45	72	0.889	0.38
Grenada	17	0.893	0.431	30	0.837	0.281	23	0.845	0.326
Guatemala	99	0.771	0.31	127	0.745	0.277	153	0.727	0.282
Guyana	32	0.88	0.472	35	0.899	0.434	55	0.885	0.35
Honduras	58	0.884	0.451	84	0.84	0.393	90	0.864	0.535
Hong Kong, China	127	0.715	0.315	174	0.649	0.146	172	0.614	0.152
India	154	0.662	0.153	207	0.632	0.142	226	0.604	0.137
Indonesia	121	0.714	0.453	198	0.699	0.269	210	0.607	0.146
Jamaica	85	0.803	0.462	81	0.857	0.64	93	0.85	0.502
Jordan	72	0.855	0.371	126	0.764	0.349	113	0.788	0.27
Kenya	104	0.823	0.34	183	0.675	0.239	174	0.735	0.231
Kuwait	127	0.729	0.57	121	0.849	0.608	131	0.914	0.94
Macau, China	93	0.844	0.552	126	0.846	0.295	135	0.828	0.315
Malaysia	158	0.612	0.266	219	0.581	0.184	227	0.52	0.178
Malta	58	0.753	0.338	88	0.78	0.407	124	0.734	0.499

Source: UNCTAD, *Handbook of International Trade and Development Statistics*
Notes: [1] *export value exceeding $50,000*
[2] *export value exceeding $100,000*
[3] *export value exceeding $100,000*

Table 2.8. **Trade in services by modes of supply, 1997**

Mode of supply category	Value ($ bn)	Cumulative share (%)
Cross-border commercial services (excl. travel)	890	41.0
Consumer movement/Travel	430	19.8
Commercial presence/Sales by foreign affiliates	820	37.8
Temporary entry/Compensation of employees	30	1.4
Total	2 170	100.0

Source: Karsenty (1999)

Table2.9. **Leading non-OECD trading countries and their participation in FDI inflows, 1981 and 1998**

Country	Leading non-OECD trading countries						Leading non-OECD recipients of FDI					
	Rank w/in non-OECD		Value		Share in world trade		Rank w/in non-OECD		Value		Share in world FDI	
	1981	1998	1981	1998	1981	1998	1981	1998	1981	1998	1981	1998
China	5	1	32.4	373.5	0.8	2.8	..	1	0.0	43.8	0.0	7.1
Russia	..	2	..	161.8	..	1.2	..	10	0.0	2.8	0.0	0.4
Malaysia	10	3	27.7	150.0	0.7	1.1	2	6	1.3	5.0	2.1	0.8
Brazil	1	4	50.7	136.4	1.3	1.0	1	2	2.5	31.9	4.3	5.2
Thailand	14	5	18.8	112.8	0.5	0.8	8	3	0.3	6.9	0.5	1.1
India	9	6	28.6	106.6	0.7	0.8	19	11	0.1	2.6	0.2	0.4
Indonesia	2	7	49.1	92.0	1.3	0.7	15	4	0.1	6.6	0.2	1.1
Philippines	15	8	18.2	75.2	0.5	0.6	12	14	0.2	1.7	0.3	0.3
Argentina	19	9	11.2	69.5	0.3	0.5	3	5	0.8	6.2	1.4	1.0
South Africa	3	10	48.5	67.1	1.2	0.5	..	32	..	0.6	..	0.1
Chile	16	11	14.1	44.4	0.4	0.3	6	7	0.4	4.6	0.6	0.8
Venezuela	4	12	38.0	38.1	1.0	0.3	11	8	0.2	4.4	0.3	0.7
Ukraine	..	13	..	36.1	..	0.3	..	24	..	0.7	..	0.1
Colombia	18	14	11.9	34.5	0.3	0.3	9	9	0.3	3.0	0.4	0.5
Egypt	13	15	19.2	33.2	0.5	0.2	4	18	0.8	1.1	1.3	0.2
Iran	11	16	27.6	31.7	0.7	0.2	..	87	0.0	0.0	0.0	0.0
Belarus	..	17	..	29.3	..	0.2	..	56	..	0.1	..	0.0
Slovak	..	18	..	28.2	..	0.2	..	30	..	0.6	..	0.1
Romania	..	19	..	22.8	..	0.2	..	12	0.0	2.0	0.0	0.3
Pakistan	20	20	9.9	22.8	0.3	0.2	18	33	0.1	0.5	0.2	0.1
Memo items												
All of above			405.9	1 666.1	10.4	12.5			7.0	126.4	11.9	20.5
All non-OECD countries			705.3	2 167.9	18.1	16.3			9.9	141.3	16.8	22.9
World			3 901.8	13 289.4	100.0	100.0			59.1	616.6	100.0	100.0

NB: In 1998, the correlation coefficient between the ranks of FDI and of trade is 0.65.
Source: World Bank, *World Development Indicators*

Notes

1 This example is cited in WTO (1998).

2 Currently, global production sharing includes the production of parts and components or assembly-type operations in such products and sectors as automobiles, semi-conductors, valves, tuners, television and radio receivers, sewing machines, calculators, computers and other office equipment, electrical machinery, power tools and parts, typewriters, cameras, optical equipment, watches, aircraft parts, telecommunication equipment, musical instruments, and of course wearing apparel and leather goods..

3 In the non-OECD economies, the size of the service sector is particularly understated by employment and national income statistics. This is so because of the reliance on household production and the large size of the informal sector, which is usually dominated by services.

4 See Guy Karsenty (2000),"Assessing Trade in Services by Mode of Supply", in Sauvé, P. and R.M. Stern, eds., GATS 2000: New Directions in Services Trade Liberalisation, Washington, D.C.: Brookings Institution Press, pp. 33-56.

5 As illustrated by recent theoretical research - Deardorff (1999) and Markusen, Rutherford and Tarr (1999) - there are strong reasons to believe that liberalisation of such services deserve priority in the negotiations because they are crucial in terms of both increasing the gains from trade in goods and reducing the costs of international fragmentation of the value chain and production sharing.

6 See Francois and Wooton (1999) for recent studies on maritime transport. Findlay and Warren (1999) comprises a series of papers exploring the magnitude of barriers to trade in telecom, financial and other services.

7 The OECD 1996 study also points out that no single pattern holds for all countries and that in eight of the seventeen countries examined GDP growth fell after the improvement in freedom of association.

8 Rogers and Swinnerton (2000) find that while in higher-productivity countries with child labour, a more equal income distribution can reduce or eliminate child labour, in low-productivity countries, a more equal distribution of income can exacerbate child labour. In the latter case, an equalising redistribution could lower the income of the highest-income families so that their children must work, without raising any other family's income by enough to enable them to take their children out of work. (The dividing line between "high" and "low" productivity economies is estimated at real GDP per worker of $10 000 - a conservatively high estimate.) Rogers and Swinnerton suggest that a policy implication one might draw from this analysis is that in low-productivity countries emphasis should be on productivity growth rather than on equity. Though, as they acknowledge, equity-inducing policies may, in certain circumstances, have the effect of raising productivity.

9 "Report on trade and environment", OCDE/GD(95)63

10 "Environmental Benefits of Removing Trade Restrictions and Distortions" (WT/CTE/W/67), p. 3.

11 The draft "Reference Manual for Integrated Assessment of Trade-Related Policies" can be found http://www.unep.org/etu.

12 *The UNEP-UNCTAD Capacity Building Task Force on Trade, Environment and Development,* A thematic Summary of the 2nd Briefing Session for Geneva Missions, Geneva, 6 June, 2000.

13 "An assessment of the environmental, economic and development benefits of further global trade liberalisation", COM/TD/ENV(2000)86, available at http://www.oecd.org/ech/index_2.htm

III. OPENNESS AND GROWTH: EVIDENCE AND POLICY

Despite the econometric difficulties of establishing beyond doubt that openness enhances growth, this Chapter will show that the weight of the evidence is quite clearly in that direction. As will be described below, there is certainly no coherent body of evidence that it is bad for growth.

A. Trade and growth – the direct evidence

During the 1990s, the conviction that openness was good for growth was fostered at least in part by some visible and well-promoted cross-country studies *e.g.* Dollar (1992), Sachs and Warner (1995), and Edwards (1998). Recently, however, these have received critical treatment from Rodriguez and Rodrik (1999), who argue, *inter alia*, that the measures of openness used in these studies are flawed and their econometrics weak. Moreover open trade (the result of trade liberalisation) is usually only one of several indicators of openness, and one which generally seems to weigh rather lightly in the overall result - *e.g.* Harrison (1996). The difficulty of establishing an empirical link between liberal trade and growth arises from at least two difficulties: first, that of measuring the actual degree of trade restrictiveness. For example, tariffs need to be aggregated, quantitative restrictions assessed and then aggregated, and the degree of enforcement measured. Second, causation is difficult to establish.

Recently, Frankel and Romer (1999) and Irwin (2000) have tried to address the latter by examining the effects of the component of openness that is independent of economic growth. This is the part of bilateral trade flows that are explained by populations, land areas, borders and distances. This component explains a significant proportion of the differences in income levels and growth performance between countries and from this we might infer a general relationship running from increased trade to increased growth. The effect is not perfectly defined numerically, but is quite significant economically. For example, at the conservative end of Frankel and Romer's range, an increase of one percentage point in the openness ratio increases both the level of income and the subsequent growth rate by around one-half of one percent per annum.[1]

Frankel and Romer correctly observe they have inferred, not proven, that the consequences of policy-induced openness are the same as those of "natural" openness. However, it is difficult to think of reasons why this should not be so if "policy" amounts just to the absence of trade barriers. This is because the absence of barriers has a clear parallel with the absence of "natural" barriers that their exogenous component of openness captures in the case of trading partners which are close by. It is not difficult, on the other hand, to imagine that artificially stimulated trade – *e.g.* via export subsidies or via discriminatory trade policies – is less beneficial.

The last point chimes with Vamvakidis' (1998) results. Using panel data for over one hundred countries he concludes that multilateral liberalisations over the period 1950-89 were associated with increases in rates of growth, while regional (discriminatory) ones were not.[2]

Direct evidence can also be gleaned from other studies by Srinivasan and Bhagwati (1999) that chide the economics profession for forgetting the issues outlined above in their enthusiasm for cross-country studies.[3] First, there are detailed case studies of particular countries, which consider a wide variety of causes and channels for growth, but frequently find openness at the very heart of the matter – for example, the NBER study summarised in Krueger (1978). Second, there are econometric time-series studies of particular countries – *e.g.* Jonsson and Subramanian (1999), which strongly suggests a growth effect in South Africa. A case in point is the experience in Chile, a country that has turned out to be one of the best advertisements for the effects of trade liberalisation on economic performance (see Box 3.1), and a useful reference to the role of concomitant policies as will be described in Section C below.

Box 3.1. Chile: stability through compensation

Until 1973 Chile appeared no different form other Latin American regimes, given to inward-looking development policies, poor macroeconomic management and distributional struggles. Following that year, the government introduced a much more market-oriented policy. It abolished non-tariff barriers and reduced tariffs from an average of 94% (with a large dispersion) to a nearly uniform 10% over the six years to 1979. Since then it has suffered a huge economic crisis (1982) and achieved a reversion to democratic institutions (1990), but it has stuck firmly to the basic philosophy of openness and has now had over a decade of strong economic growth. As a result it has transformed its average income levels and dramatically reduced poverty.

The key elements of the story appear to be: a clear vision mediated by consultation and pragmatic implementation.

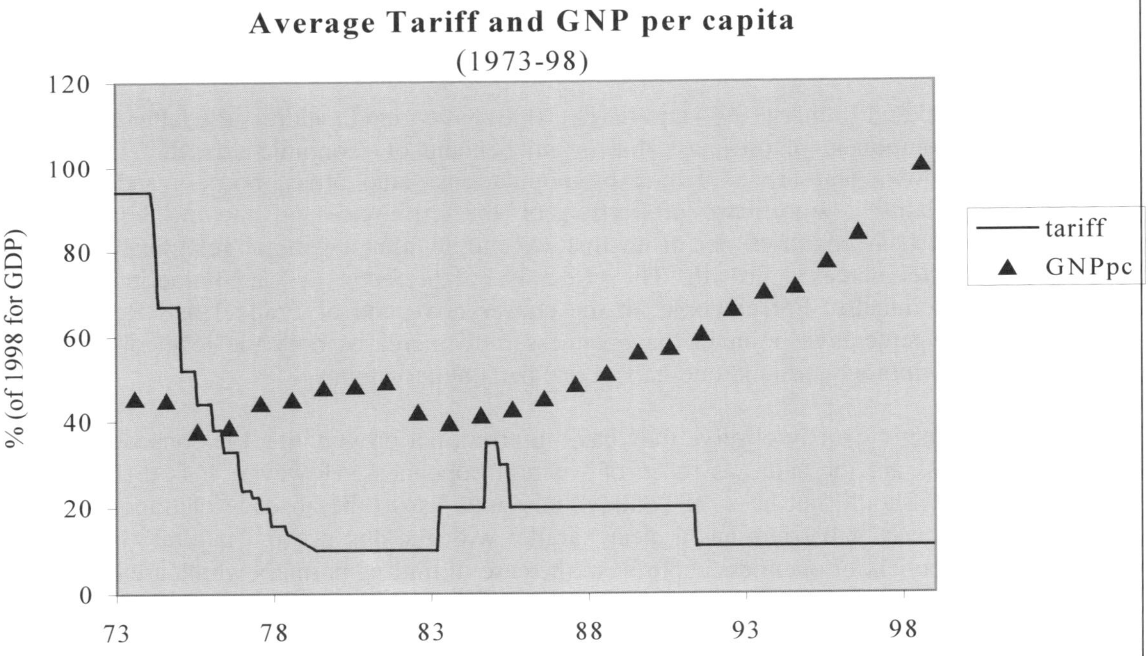

N.B. The figure above shows the progress of tariff liberalisation and economic growth since 1973.

While the government had planned to open the economy up from the very beginning, its ultimate objectives were however not particularly ambitious by today's standards – a uniform 30% tariff by some indefinite future date. Nonetheless, the starting point was so distorted that the initial liberalisation was rapid right

Box 3.1. Chile: stability through compensation (cont.)

from the start, with NTBs and tariffs falling quickly. Within its overall strategy, the government consulted widely about the shape of the reform, which undoubtedly increased the legitimacy of the process and allowed the more precise identification of interests that had to be appeased. During this phase, the main explicit compensatory policy was a severe real exchange rate depreciation (by 150% by late-1976 relative to 1973) plus a crawling peg to keep it low, which the government explicitly linked to the liberalisation of import markets. The depreciation clearly cushioned the blow for import competing interests and offered big opportunities for export and potential export sectors. The government pursued labour market reforms to increase flexibility, which benefited all commercial interests. In addition, there were a number of specific concessions such as tax rebates and subsidies to appease certain sectors, including traditional agricultural producers.

The early stages of tariff reform appeared to generate less opposition than had been anticipated – presumably because of the compensation and the fact that non-traditional exports boomed. Thus, after 1976 the government became more confident and initiated the push for a low uniform tariff. It also stated publicly that uniformity was necessary to prevent the capture of the protection system by special interests.

This first phase ended in 1979, following a change in macro-stabilisation policy and the introduction of wage indexation, both of which contributed to a strong real appreciation. Over the next three years the exchange rate became quite unsustainable and resulted in the balance of payments crisis, during which GDP fell by 14% in 1982 alone. The crisis led to a progressive raising of the uniform tariff (to 35% by September 1984), a 120-day financing requirement for imports and to a number of ad hoc import surcharges. The last, imposed in response to private sector requests, must be seen as fundamentally political in nature. Thus trade liberalisation was essentially in retreat over this period, but it did not turn into a rout because, according to De la Cuadra and Hachette (1991), the government maintained the main principles of its trade regime – non-discrimination and no non-tariff barriers. The large depreciation engendered by the crisis helped the traded goods industries weather the storm and by 1984 recovery was starting.

From here on, economic performance has been strong and the government actually pursued rather few explicitly compensatory measures. The tariff was reduced to 20% in mid-1985 (thus the emergency rate applied for only 9 months) and to 15% in mid-1988. The democratic government which came to power in March 1990 adjusted a number of elements of economic policy, but, perhaps to signal its commitment to the market, reduced the tariff to 11% in mid-1991. The willingness of the new regime to continue the trade liberalisation shows how widely accepted it had become politically, which, in turn, was almost certainly a major factor in its durability and effectiveness.

Chilean experience suggests a number of lessons for a successful trade liberalisation:

- Even a dictatorial regime felt that it needed to pay attention to private sector demands: except for left-wing organised labour, other groups were consulted and offered compensation of various sorts to keep them 'on board'.
- Compensation was important – especially via the exchange rate, which was an explicit instrument of policy for much of the period.
- In some cases direct pay-offs in terms of added protection were offered to certain groups, but the basic principles were maintained and the reversal of policy was relatively short-lived.
- Successive governments were encouraged by the broad public support to continue the policies that were established in the late 1970s. This gave the policy regime a sturdiness, which almost certainly enhanced its effectiveness.
- Uniformity (even de facto imperfect uniformity) offered a useful bulwark against political pressures. It also enhanced transparency.
- *Source*: Edwards and Lederman (1999).

B. Trade and growth – the indirect evidence

The indirect evidence examines empirically the steps in the causal relationship between trade and growth. The main issue is the *productivity* effect. Tybout (2000) offers a good account of the productivity effects of openness on manufacturing industry in non-OECD countries. Again this is a bit mixed, but it certainly does not suggest adverse effects. The evidence suggests that openness effects operate more through import barriers – *e.g.* Esfahani (1991) and Feenstra *et al.* (1997) – than through exports (see Box 3.2).

The frequently quoted Coe, Helpman and Hoffmaister (1997) study suggests that import links to OECD countries are a key determinant of non-OECD countries' productivity growth, but it is not definitive. They hypothesise that trade in capital goods provides the link between OECD countries' R&D and non-OECD countries' total factor productivity (TFP), but they do not test it at all formally. Almost certainly they could not reject any of several other plausible links related to openness, and commenting on earlier intra-OECD work, Keller (1999) suggests that they could not reject the hypothesis that the links are completely random. It is perhaps not surprising that the effects of trade reforms are difficult to isolate statistically, since trade liberalisation is rarely implemented as a stand-alone policy measure, nor is such a course recommended. It has long been accepted that trade liberalisation needs companion policies to be successful, often including other market reforms, macroeconomic stabilisation, exchange rate adjustment, and adequate safety nets.

Box 3.2. Uganda: When paying tariffs sometimes beats not paying them

Among African economies over the last 15 years, Uganda has emerged as an important exemplar of good policy. Its policy reforms have been wide-ranging and deep, but two of their most important aspects have been the dramatic reduction in export taxes and the restoration of reliability and predictability to the tax and regulatory system. Where very high tariffs (and other non-tariff barriers) were once reserved for the few who lacked the negotiating skills and political muscle to avoid them, Uganda has moved to a system of relatively low tariffs applied even-handedly with few exemptions. Suddenly business knows where it stands relative both to reaping its profits and to facing up to uncomfortable foreign competition. The growth pay-off has been remarkable, with GDP doubling over eleven years (1986-97). And as the figure below shows, this has been achieved with relatively little change in (and more or less no relationship to) the share of GDP exported (*X/GDP*) and while the average tax-take on imports (a measure of average tariffs, *avg. tariff*) has risen strongly. Despite the reduction in export taxes, the overall combined revenue from tariffs and export taxes as a percentage of GDP *(tr tax/GDP)* remained fairly stable.

Box 3.2. Uganda: When paying tariffs sometimes beats not paying them (cont.)

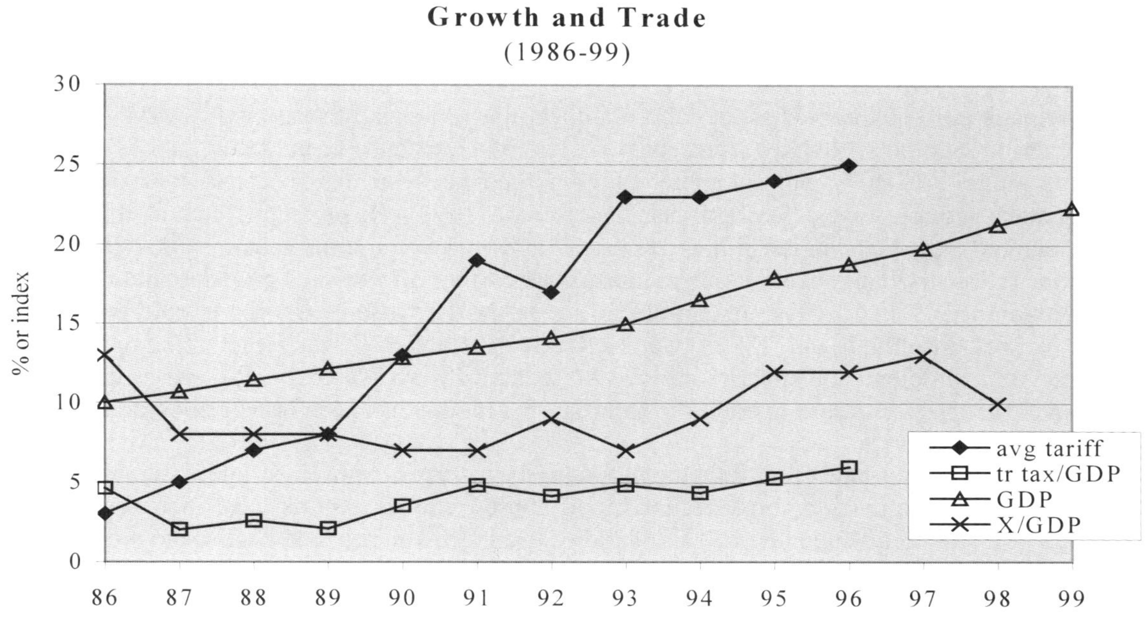

N.B. For presentational convenience GDP is scaled such that 1986 = 10. *Source* (for the figure above): Bigsten (2000).

Uganda has quite clearly got a huge distance to go in the race for development; its GNP per head is still only $320 (WDI, 2000). And its location is such a handicap in the modern world, that there is at least a possibility that it will never attain the very highest levels of income per head. Being land-locked – especially by countries whose infrastructure and transportation efficiency are not of the highest order – means that Uganda has a large degree of natural protection, or expressed differently, will never be as completely integrated into the world economy as many other countries.[4] [This is especially true given its continuing high levels of tax on fuels.] Nevertheless, by a series of sound policy measures, including a willingness to engage seriously with the rest of the world despite its natural isolation, Uganda is now moving itself off the lowest developmental rung. It is increasing its integration by removing unnecessary policy barriers to trade and reducing its own trading costs via customs and transportation reform, and as a result has stimulated its productive efficiency and increased economic growth.A key element in the rehabilitation of the Ugandan economy was its relative stability macroeconomically since 1987 (with a small reversal in 1991). This was true of monetary policy, fiscal policies and, critically, exchange rate policy, in which huge black market premia were gradually reduced to nothing. The last, of course, represented a large *de facto* opening of the economy, for it made international trade both more attractive (to exporters) and more predictable. At the same time internal marketing and price reforms allowed market forces freer reign in the exportable commodities sectors (especially coffee in which over 100 private firms entered the trading business when the official monopsony was abolished). Associated with the latter was a reduction in export taxes, from over 30% of exports in 1986 to virtually nothing by 1998.

Box 3.2. Uganda: When paying tariffs sometimes beats not paying them (cont.)

Similarly, import policy was gradually reformed both to reduce trade restrictions and to increase the reliability and consistency of policy: to replace a regime of *ad hoc* and sometimes *ad hominem* interventions with one of transparency, consistency and relative non-corruption. It was arguably the reliability of the regime rather than the level of average of tariffs that was the key. As the figure above shows, average tariffs expressed as the ratio of collections to the value of imports showed a strong rise over the period, but they probably represented far less of a barrier to actual trade. In 1987, most tariffs lay in the range 10%-40%, but a number of items had rates up to 350% and most imports faced discriminatory indirect taxes (Dean, Desai and Reidel, 1994). However, in fact at that time most imports entered duty-free under either formal or informal exemption schemes. In 1989 the tariff regime was rationalised and exemptions reduced, with further reforms in 1992 (maximum tariff 60%), 1996 (maximum 30%) and 1997 (maximum 20%). In the 1998 Budget, a three-band tariff (0%, 7% and 15%) was instituted and NTBs were effectively abolished altogether. Exemptions remain something of a problem and discriminatory excise taxes were levied on imports, especially from Kenya, over the late 1990s, but overall, the nature of the regime has been transformed dramatically.

In terms of trade performance, total factor productivity in firms exposed to international competition has increased as trade barriers have declined, and non-traditional exports have increased strongly to reach 29% of export revenue by 1999. Overall export growth has not been exceptionally strong, however, possibly because remaining barriers penalise exporting relative to domestic sales (with negative effective protection) or because of the economy's natural protection, or because of external trade barriers. But the benefits of reform are felt not just through quantities but via the market information and competitive stimulus provided by exposure to world markets. The critical element in this first phase of Uganda's recovery is almost certainly the reliability with which such signals arrive rather than the precise level of any wedge that government policy adds to them. Price signals are no longer subject to arbitrary reversal by policy intervention: firms can plan on accessing imports if they can pay for them and no longer see lobbying as a more cost-effective option than adapting to market pressures. (Source: Bigstein, 2000).

C. Trade liberalisation is not sufficient: are there necessary concomitants?

While liberal trade policies are likely to be beneficial under any circumstances (because they enlarge the set of opportunities for economic agents), a quasi-permanent effect on growth almost certainly requires combination with other good policies as well. The latter point is made by the Bretton Woods institutions in their policy advice, although Mosley (2000) argues that their attempts to prove it have not been very successful.[5] One vital concomitant to trade policy is development co-operation --that dimension is considered separately in Chapter VI below.

(i) Trade, governance and growth: regulatory reform

A decade ago Krueger (1990) argued that openness is likely to be correlated with better policy in a number of dimensions, but empirical work on this is very much at its early stages. In 1997, the OECD Trade Committee identified a series of principles for ensuring that the domestic regulatory process does not distort resource allocation, productive efficiency and ultimately international competition while ensuring governments' ability to regulate and to meet economic and non-economic policy objectives. For instance, improved transparency of domestic policy making enhances the security and predictability of the market, allowing well-informed production and investment decisions and safeguarding the equality of competitive opportunities among market participants. Regulatory approaches that are not more trade restrictive than necessary to fulfil legitimate policy objectives not only facilitate international competition but at the same time free up domestic productive resources that were previously needed to meet cumbersome regulatory requirements. Reliance on internationally harmonised standards as the basis for domestic regulations facilitates the access of new and innovative foreign products to the domestic market as well as enhances the market opportunities of domestic firms and products world-wide. At the same time, improved regulatory practices may fall short of their promise in terms of market access and productive efficiency if they fail to control anti-competitive private behaviour, hence the importance of associating an effective application of competition principles.

1. Overall, reviews of regulatory reform in OECD countries have shown that good governance at home can enhance the openness of domestic markets to domestic and foreign competitors alike while favouring the growth of FDI and trade as well as the development of internationally competitive business. Revealing examples can be seen in certain service sectors such as telecommunications and transportation, where competition-inhibiting barriers tend to be relatively high (see above, Box 2.1). The reduction of regulatory barriers in these sectors accelerates infrastructure development that is essential for growth in other productive sectors and suppresses launching and operation costs related both to regulation and to market conditions.

(ii) Trade, governance and growth: corruption

Another critical dimension of good governance is *corruption*: recent evidence from Ades and Di Tella (1997, 1999) shows a clear cross-country connection between higher rents, stemming from things such as active industrial policy or low degrees of openness, and higher corruption. The latter, in turn, reduces investment and hence growth. Wei (2000), however, suggests another reason for the corruption-openness link: open countries face greater losses from corruption than less open ones, because corruption impinges disproportionately on foreign transactions. As a result they have greater incentives to develop better institutions. He finds evidence for this theory in two cross-country relationships. First, corruption is correlated with "natural openness" (essentially the Frankel-Romer variable, which is exogenous) but not with "residual openness" (*i.e.* the difference between actual and natural openness, which is probably related to policies). Second, more open countries pay their civil servants better, suggesting that they value better administration more highly (although there may be difficulties over the direction of causation here).

There is a multitude of studies linking corruption with poor economic performance, and as noted above, recent research has started to explore the links between openness and corruption. The cross-country regressions that underlie that work are very good for describing data and perhaps even for suggesting causal connections, but their high levels of aggregation and their imprecision about measurement leave policy-makers feeling exposed when it comes to making concrete reforms.

Important research work on corruption over the nineties - the "corruption-eruption" in Doig and Riley's (1998) phrase – agrees on at least two things. First, corruption is a complex phenomenon subject to a great deal of country-specific variation in cause and manifestation. While there are commonalities, they exist at the level of general principles rather than off-the-shelf policy prescriptions - for example, that corruption is positively related to the degree of bureaucratic discretion. Second, corruption is systemic and pervades many parts of the afflicted societies. It is not merely a matter of corrupt individuals but of systemic failure and must be addressed as such. Thus corruption needs to be tackled on a broad front, and the key ingredient is "strong political will demonstrated by a commitment from the leadership at all levels of government" (Kpundeh, 1998).

The breadth required for this task is illustrated by a recent survey of OECD countries (OECD, 1999). This showed that every OECD country operates a wide range of different anti-corruption policies/approaches, including regulation and law on corruption, investigative bodies, ombudsmen, training for public officials and tight financial management. But the results of this study also suggest two other important observations: that merely having policies in place is not sufficient to ensure low levels of corruption, and that one needs to address the policy environment in which corruption flourishes.

On the former – whether having policies on the books is sufficient - the correlations between the number of policies adopted by different OECD countries and their (admittedly imperfect) rankings in corruption league-tables are not strongly positive.

Kaufmann (1998) particularly stresses the second observation above about the policy environment - that one must address the incentives for corruption. This is a key and often unappreciated element of anti-corruption policy, which goes to the heart of the disease rather than merely dealing with its symptoms. Kaufmann also stresses the need to avoid biases in the implementation phase of anti-corruption policy, such as:

- Anti-business bias.
- Tackling symptoms (*e.g.* the number of arrests) rather than fundamental causes.
- Ex post focus rather than an ex ante one.
- Quick-fix bias, looking into immediate causes rather than fundamental but indirect ones.
- Injection bias – introducing new schemes and institutions rather than correcting existing ones.
- Anti-counterfactual bias – assessing institutions without properly asking what would have happened to corruption without them, but with, say, the same changes in the underlying environment.
- Prose-bias – using proclamations rather than evidence.
- Toolkit bias – as opposed to tailoring approaches to local circumstances.
- Christmas tree bias – too much fine-tuning and detail, and
- Anti-economic reform bias – not recognising the way that distortionary economic policies create scope for corruption.

Although the issue of corruption has not been addressed in the WTO Agreements, WTO disciplines can contribute indirectly to anti-corruption efforts by promoting good governance in member countries. In enforcing their WTO obligations, member countries will simultaneously reduce the opportunities and motivations for corruption, thus making corruption less likely to occur. This mainly concerns corruption in international transactions, but the achievement of a more transparent, predictable and less arbitrary regulatory environment can also reduce corruption in domestic transactions. However, although appropriate trade policy can contribute to a general anti-corruption drive and benefit from other elements of such a drive, it can only ever be one part of the overall strategy.

The less restrictive trade policy is, the lower the incentives for corruption: the returns to avoiding a 5% tariff are lower than those to avoiding a 50% tariff, so the former gives customs officers or more senior officials less scope for extracting rent. Second, a simple, transparent and non-discretionary trade policy reduces the scope for corruption. Thus even if tariffs exist, there are important benefits to their being uniform (or at most having very few bands), keeping them stable, and to publishing them. Quantitative restrictions (QRs) are certainly second-best from a transparency perspective, but similarly, if they must exist, they should be publicly auctioned and clearly documented. For both tariffs and QRs, the geographical dimension is important: uniformity over sources of imports is at least as important as uniformity over types of import, for the origin of a good is often less easy to check (and hence more liable to falsification) than its nature. The rules of origin that accompany preferential liberalisation are burdensome to the honest trader and a great opportunity for less honest ones.

This advice is not new – it has been standard fare in the World Bank and other international bodies for two decades. But it is still frequently violated. The classic success case is Chile, a country that transformed its economic performance and its public administrative standards in dealing with corruption over two decades. As mentioned in Box 3.1 above, Chile abolished QRs and reduced tariffs from very high and variable rates to a virtually uniform 10% over the period 1974-79. Moreover, although the economic crisis of the early 1980s required, or at least led to, dramatic increases in tariffs (up to 35% in 1984), uniformity was maintained, and the various steps in the de-escalation back to 11% in 1991 pre-announced and faithfully implemented.

At a more general, but less concrete level, Gatti (1999) makes the argument for uniformity and shows that corruption in trade administration is positively associated with the variance of tariff rates across commodities. The direction of causation is not clear in this work, but theory strongly suggests that uniform tariffs will aid the fight against corruption, so even if the causation runs the other way, uniformity will be a useful indicator of countries' progress towards greater integrity.

However, even a zero tariff does not remove the discretion of customs and other officials (including whoever assesses conformity to technical regulations, food safety, etc.) because goods must satisfy various standards requirements. Customs reform is frequently an important part of the trade-anti-corruption link (see Box 3.3). Stasavage and Daubree's (1997) study of Mali and Senegal identified trade reforms as a key input into the reduction of customs fraud. They also called attention to the need to ensure that customs officials had the means to do their jobs and maintain reasonable livelihoods. They argued that in these two countries poor civil service pay was less of a problem than the insufficiency of funds for non-wage expenditure (vehicles, fuel, etc.).

All of the points discussed here figure in World Bank (2000), which recommends concrete anti-corruption policies for Bangladesh. This publication estimates that annual underpayment of customs duties costs the government between $100 and $200 million per year, and that inefficiency in the port of Chittagong (much of which appears to be intended to set up scope for additional payments) costs a further $500 million to $1 billion per year economically.

Most of the countries that have been successful at addressing corruption have instituted high-level watch-dog institutions – *e.g.* Hong Kong-China, Singapore, Chile, Botswana and Malaysia. Given the importance of incentives, such institutions are not sufficient, but they seem to be part of the strategy. Obviously such watch-dogs survey more than just trading institutions, but equally, neither must trade be allowed to avoid their gaze. Trade involves foreign firms (and even governments) and poses its own particular technical issues, so it is somewhat different from domestic activity. However, the basic requirement for honesty is just as important and the watch-dog must subject the trade sector to at least the same set of tests as it uses for other parts of the economy.

To conclude, however, as well as watch-dogs, successful anti-corruption campaigns are also associated with economic regimes or reforms that reduce bureaucratic discretion and increase the scope for the market.

Box 3.3. Reforming customs administration

The professionalisation of the customs service, with appropriate recruitment practices, strong internal codes of ethics, association to an external professional body and proper career and promotion procedures based on merit can do a lot to reinforce good practice. The World Customs Organisation (WCO) offers codes and advice and provides professional support to customs officials whose organisations invite them to assist. They have a fair measure of success and should figure in the plans for any serious customs reform. On the ground, press reports suggest that part of the success of the Ugandan Revenue Authority in cleaning up its act was due to its explicit effort to recruit from religious groups whose beliefs offered external support to the notion of ethical behaviour. At the other extreme, another World Bank anecdote tells of a country, with income per head at current exchange rates of around $400 per head, in which the right to job in customs traded at $40,000.

One immediate action in an attempt to improve customs performance is often to employ Pre-Shipment Inspection (PSI) service firms, which essentially help evaluate customs duties prior to export in the exporting country. In most cases these are not used as the collection medium for actual taxes, but they can provide the informational basis such as valuation and/or standards information. More often, however, they are used as a way of monitoring local customs performance, by, for example, predicting the amounts of duty due.

PSI firms have clearly had an important role in meeting immediate crises – for example in Indonesia – and have been an important part of Bretton Woods lending conditionality in Africa. But they are certainly not free from controversy. First, they are relatively costly, and so must pay for themselves in terms of additional revenue collected. Second, they have been subject to corruption themselves and the award of contracts has sometimes been dubious. Third, PSI *per se* is a council of despair about improving local accountability; in the absence of training, it does nothing to improve local customs or to contribute to the general anti-corruption drive. Indeed, by externalising enforcement, it possibly reduces local restraint – corruption merely becomes a game against foreigners rather than an expropriation of local incomes.

Fourth and most importantly, PSI will achieve nothing if its findings are not acted upon. If PSI companies identify serious under-collection of duty or unjustified barriers to imports (that are probably designed just to elicit bribes), governments have to act against the customs officials concerned. Far too often they do not, so PSI becomes one of Kaufmann's pieces of window-dressing rather than serious attempt to address corruption.[6]

(iii) Trade, governance and growth: politics

Good governance is not just about curbing illegal activity; it is also about whether legal activity is conducive to good outcomes. This observation is as pertinent to the field of trade policy as to any other. International trade policy is strongly redistributive – the transfers between actors are generally much larger than the net effects on overall economic welfare. Thus protection transfers real income from consumers to producers, and from unprotected producers to protected ones. Regional trading arrangements typically transfer tariff revenue from the government in one partner country to producers in another. In addition, trade policy is generally technical and arcane, so it does not take much to keep it out of the public gaze.

A good deal of research into the origins and nature of international trade policy – most of it for OECD countries - has identified opacity as one of the principal attractions to policy makers. For example, Finger, Hall and Nelson (1982) initiated a huge literature on anti-dumping policy and other safeguards measures. Their work stressed the attractions to all actors of keeping the granting of protection out of the political limelight. And the situation is no different 20 years on. Finger (1981) develops a general argument about the benefits of obscurantism. Similarly, the attractions of using Voluntary Export Restraints to curtail imports lay substantially in their ability to keep domestic constituencies ignorant of the costs they were bearing: no domestic institutions were required to administer them, and tracing their economic effects was complex for non-economists.

There are two practical implications of these observations about trade policy. First, while higher barriers are worse than lower ones – they create higher rents and permit greater inefficiency – the variability of barriers is probably more important from a growth perspective. Putting aside the administrative arguments (see above) there is an economic argument for mild variability across commodities (because elasticities of demand for imports vary); but the variation should not be too large or too arbitrary. One of the main nails in the coffin of import substitution polices was the discovery, in the 1970s, of just how indefensibly large and arbitrary these variances had become.

The more pernicious variance is through time for any particular commodity. First, such variability precludes rational planning by producers and consumers and so will hit investment. Second, the variance will not be random, but in response to requests for protection from producers – or sometimes requests for tariff reductions by using industries.[7] If these favours are regularly granted, firms will find it more profitable to lobby than to address competition in more constructive ways and the whole dynamic of the economy will be undermined. Thus in the old import substitution regimes, it was probably the constant and endogenous tinkering with the regime that most undermined economic performance. Since tinkering is easier if there are no bindings and if tariffs are high enough to allow plenty of room for movement, stability and reliability in the protection regime tend to be associated with more liberal regimes.

The second observation is that there is a prominent bias in trade policy making towards producer interests and away from consumers'. In many societies, production is seen as an objective rather than a means to an end (good living) and as virtuous in contrast to indulgent consumption. In addition, because firms specialise, they have narrow but deep interests and so find it worthwhile to lobby whenever they are threatened; consumers, on the other hand, only ever have a small interest in any particular act of trade policy because they spend their incomes on such a wide variety of goods and services. Firms also find it easier to organise lobbying, because they are far fewer in number than consumers and hence can overcome the problem of free-riding (letting someone else bear the cost of a common good). At the extreme, where only business interests seem to matter, one might characterise this as state-capture.

Good governance entails establishing institutions and procedures that insulate trade policy from day-to-day business pressures (see Box 3.4). That is, while trade policy should be business friendly in the large and in the long run, it should be business-resistant in its details. This can be achieved among other things by:

- Allowing the legislature full oversight of trade policy but not to manipulate its detail.
- Offering to trade policymakers an advocacy role in favour of market openness in the context of sectoral policies.

- Improving the accountability of the executive order over trade policy by introducing publicly available cost-benefit/impact analysis and holding wide consultations with consumers and users. And

- by considering the overall policy package, including available alternatives when assessing the trade impact of proposed policies and regulations --low MFN tariffs or tight safeguards procedures will not maintain a liberal trade regime, to the extent that anti-dumping is abused.

Box 3.4. Trade policy should be business friendly but not business-owned

As noted in the text, trade policy should be business friendly in the large and in the long run, but business-resistant in its details. A number of recommendations to help this exist in the economics literature. In particular, work by Winters (1995), which formulated advice on trade policy institutions to transition economies, contains the following recommendations:

- Allow the legislature full oversight of trade policy, but not to manipulate its detail. The notorious Smoot-Hawley tariff of 1929 was the result of legislative tariff setting: every Congressmen bid for protection for his own constituents and as a price for getting that did nothing to hinder his colleagues form getting protection for theirs. Within the legislature, sound committee structures and legislative practices can help to promote good policy.
- Let the executive determine the details of trade policy, but ensure that it bears both the political costs and benefits of protection. Avoid establishing institutions behind which the executive can shelter if consumers do object to protection. [These shelters are things like anti-dumping bodies, which allow the executive to say to consumers, 'but it was all perfectly legal that X was protected. I could do nothing,' while saying to producers 'we have a system that allows me to meet your needs.']
- Avoid using sectoral ministries to determine trade policy. For example, almost everywhere the Minister of Agriculture's job is seen as ensuring the health of (domestic) agriculture: they are not well established to see the benefits of freer trade (or of rigorous health regulations). Run trade policy from a dedicated senior ministry with access to, but not allegiance to, Finance and Foreign Affairs.
- Recognise the substitutability between instruments: low MFN tariffs or tight safeguards procedures will not maintain a liberal trade regime if the anti-dumping gate is wide open to petitioners.
- Similarly, regional free trade is not the same thing as free trade.
- If anti-dumping policies are politically necessary, require the authorities to hear from consumers and users, and require them to justify interventions in the national interest explicitly including consumer interests.
- Require non-tariff measures to be justified explicitly.
- Give trade law fairly high status legally, so that it can not readily be changed by low-level officials. Require periodic reports to the legislature, so that voters can monitor the overall trade stance.
- Pay the costs of a body to protect consumer interests - *e.g.* reviewing trade policy, preparing the free trade case in anti-dumping suits - a sort of official opposition. And ensure that it is free of political interference by guaranteeing funds for a long period. Allow this body to initiate debate about the case for freer trade.

(iv) Trade, governance and growth: policy concomitants

a. Investment

Investment lies at the centre of Rodrik's (1995, 1997) view of the Asian miracle: it was due to strong incentives to invest (policy or otherwise) increasing both imports of capital goods and the supply of exports with which to pay for them. He argues that direct export incentives, via subsidies or devaluation, could not explain Korea's or Taiwan's export booms because they did not vary much. It is not correct, however, to infer from this that openness did not matter. Srinivasan and Bhagwati (1999) note that openness (*i.e.* decent export incentives) was the *sine qua non* of investment because one needs to sell the output on large markets where it will not drive prices down. And similarly, if markets for imported capital equipment had not been open, the whole process would never have got underway. This is a more nuanced view of openness and growth than many, but not a fundamentally antipathetic one. It chimes with the need to ensure that investment is both attractive and feasible if you want to grow, a view that leads one to think of property rights, peace and financial depth as necessary conditions.

b. Conflict resolution

Rodrik (1997, 1999) has extended the argument from investment to political and social conditions. He argues that the critical distinguishing variable between high and low growth countries is their ability to manage tension and conflict. Growth inevitably entails change and this will be easier if economic agents feel less threatened and accord greater legitimacy to the process of change (see Box 3.5). He argues that institutions to manage such conflicts are generally strong in East Asia and in the OECD countries and weaker in Latin America and Africa. Clearly such institutions could have an independent effect on growth by encouraging co-operation and flexibility. But they may also interact strongly with openness, for the latter is a major source of change; indeed, it depends on change for its beneficial effects. That is, successful openness may require good conflict resolution.

An outcome of conflict resolution is the distribution of income. Kuznet's postulated invert-U-shaped relationship between growth (development) and income distribution (rising at first, then falling) has received rather little empirical support. The dominant current view is that growth does not have any necessary implications for distribution – *e.g.* Dollar and Kraay (2000). And more recently, scholars have started to argue that the causal relationship runs in the opposite direction - *e.g.* Aghion, Caroli and Garcia-Penasola (1999), Benabou (1996). Thus, a relatively equal distribution is seen as a boon for growth, although whether this is independent of factors such as broad education and decent dispute resolution is less clear. There is a possible interaction with trade liberalisation here. There is no evidence that trade liberalisation is generally bad for income inequality - *e.g.* Dollar and Kraay (2000) - but there will quite clearly be cases where this is so (Winters, 2000). In particular, one thinks of economies whose comparative advantage lies in land or capital intensive goods –. *e.g.* much of Latin America and Africa, (Spillembergo and others, 2000). In these economies there is a clear need to manage the distributional effects of liberalisation through compensatory policy in order to reap the maximum benefit from openness.

Box 3.5. Institutions for growth: conflict resolution

It is now widely recognised that institutions play a pivotal role in economic growth and development. In the main text above, we described institutions designed to promote and preserve a liberal trade policy. Here we examine briefly what is known about institutions for promoting growth. Early contributions on these issues came from luminaries such as Douglass North and Mancur Olsen among others, but in the context of openness and growth the main protagonist has been Rodrik.

Rodrik (1999a) – graphically entitled 'where did all the growth go?' – parsimoniously captures the role in institutions in the following way (this description is based on Rodrik, 1999b):

*Changes in growth = -external shock * (latent social conflict / institutions of conflict management)*

External shocks are represented in a number of ways, but most obviously by the change in the terms of trade, latent social conflict by either income inequality or ethnic fractionalisation, and institutions of conflict management by democracy, the rule of law or public spending on social insurance.

This equation postulates that the change in growth is a function of the size of shocks faced by economies arbitrated by their ability to deal with them. Latent social conflict increases the burden of negative shocks, frequently, Rodrik argues, greatly magnifying the effect of the shock on income. That is, a shock costing x% can end up costing several times that in terms of lost income if it induces destructive political frictions or even stalemate in political management. Counteracting the degree of friction, however, are institutions designed to manage shocks, which can greatly reduce the effect. When functioning well, these institutions allow societies to make the adjustments necessary to accommodate the shocks quickly and without costly side-squabbles. They have two roles in Rodrik's view. First, they ease the pain of adjustment, possibly spreading it out so that no section of society feels that it is bearing a disproportionate share. Second, they legitimise decisions (implicit or explicit) that certain parts of society must bear costs, so that social costs can be borne without leading to social or political collapse.

The estimates, based on a cross-section of countries, suggest varying degrees of evidence in favour of the maintained hypotheses. After allowing for a number of known factors determining economic growth, Rodrik finds the expected relationships between the postulated variables and change in economic growth between 1960-75 and 1975-89.

In a later paper Rodrik (2000) addresses the question of what institutions matter and how to achieve them. On the former issue he identifies five critical areas:

- Property rights – strictly speaking, control over property rather than legal rights *per se*;
- Regulatory institutions to correct externalities, information failures and market power – such as anti-trust bodies, banking supervision and, more controversially, co-ordination of major investment decisions as Rodrik argues was provided by Korean and Taiwanese economic intervention;
- Institutions for macroeconomic stabilisation – *e.g.* a lender of last resort;
- Social Insurance – these are often transfer programmes, but Rodrik argues that other institutions such as jobs-for-life can also play the same role; and
- Institutions to manage social conflict as discussed above.

Box 3.5. Institutions for growth: conflict resolution (cont.)

On the latter issue of how to acquire institutions, Rodrik makes two observations:

- There is no single optimal set of institutions – there are many ways of achieving the same objectives. Moreover, the interactions between institutions mean that the package needs to be considered as a whole (or at most in a few broad parts) rather than piece by piece.

- Institutions can be adopted from abroad or evolved by trial and error locally. Rodrik prefers the latter, although he recognises that it often provides political cover for an unwillingness to reform and that it takes time and can involve blind alleys.

The critical issue here is the legitimacy of the institutions. Adopting foreign institutions can often be an efficient way of short-cutting the learning process, and indeed good policy-making will always seek to learn from others' experience. The requirement, however, is that the institutions be sought as solutions to *locally identified* problems and be *adapted to local needs and conditions* in quite subtle ways. There is world of difference between a society facing a problem and looking abroad for something to adapt to its own needs, and an external force declaring that such-and- such an institution will be good for it.

At least part of the job of institutions is to codify solutions to distributional conflicts – to codify trade-offs. Institutions help to ensure that the same rules apply through time, and thus make it easier for losers in 'issue A' to accept their loses because they believe that on future 'issue B' they will reap corresponding gains. But institutions can only assist in finding such solutions if, broadly speaking, they push in the direction in which society wishes to go anyway.

Rodrik goes on to argue that while we (in particular he means international financial institutions) should not impose specific institutional structures on countries, it would be reasonable to insist on basic human rights and democracy. He adduces some evidence that while democracy neither significantly raises nor reduces mean rates of economic growth, it is associated with greater stability in growth, investment and consumption, better responses to negative shocks and more equal distributions of (a) personal income and (b) rents between labour and capital. He concludes of democracy that '[i]f there is one area where institutional conditionality is both appropriate and of great economic value ...this is it.'

There are two caveats to this conclusion. First, while participatory government and democracy are to be lauded, it is not clear that the international community, let alone international financial institutions, have the right to insist on them. If, in Rodrik's phrase, democracy is a 'meta-institution', this would be meta-conditionality: it would be interference of the deepest kind, and it could undermine the legitimacy of governments and their willingness to interact with the international community at all.

Second, other scholars have worried more than Rodrik about the causality in all this. Clague et al (1997) observe that the factors associated with lasting democracy – *e.g.* equality, racial harmony, clean bureaucracy –are also associated with better economic policy directly. Clague et al identify regime stability as an important dimension of the pro-growth environment and note that switches from democracy to autocracy tend to be associated with improving property rights (their touchstone of institutional support for economic growth). In other words, while the call to democracy is doubtless uplifting and something one might encourage within countries, it is far from proven as a tool for the international community to wield in the search for economic development.

c. *Education*

Education is probably near the top of any *a priori* list of the causes of economic growth, although simple exercises that entail sticking education into cross-country growth equations have not proved very convincing. The role of education is multi-dimensional. It is likely to induce flexibility (education imparts transferable skills). It brings its own rewards in terms of productivity, so that increasing human capital will lead to increased output. Education also appears to have strong payoffs in terms of health (and social capital). Finally, it is almost certainly necessary to facilitate the absorption of new technologies (Abramovitz and David, 1996). Since in the long run technology is the key to sustained growth – merely accumulating human or physical capital will eventually encounter diminishing returns – this argument is clearly key. It is also crucial in the context of openness, for this too is felt to operate primarily by opening up the economy to new technologies. Education is therefore likely to be another necessary concomitant for openness to bring continuing dynamic benefits.

A potentially important dimension of this question for non-OECD countries is whether openness stimulates the demand for education or not. Simple Stolper-Samuelson theory would suggest that, as a skill-scarce economy opens up, the returns to skill will decline, and with them the incentives for education. Hence one needs a slightly more sophisticated view of the economy to maintain any optimism in this respect. Multi-dimensional Stolper-Samuelson, endogenous growth with constant returns to R&D, a skills-bias in tradables as opposed to non-tradables would all do the trick.

Related to the supply of educated labour is the need not to waste it in directly unproductive activities (DUPs). The traditional DUP activities such as excessive regulation, evading regulation, lobbying and litigation are all skill intensive, and their negative association with economic growth is well established. Intense interaction with the international community in the form of attendance at international meetings or negotiating technical standards or trade agreements is also skill intensive. It is important for non-OECD countries to represent their interests properly in a multilateral world, but it is equally important to remember that real economic progress occurs at home. The international community must beware of over-compensating the current under-representation of non-OECD countries by establishing procedures that absorb too much skilled labour. It is incumbent on everybody to ensure that participation is cost-effective: OECD countries by designing international institutions in which non-OECD countries can intervene effectively but cheaply, and non-OECD countries by adopting efficient strategies such as selecting issues on which to intervene carefully, adopting ready-made standards and institutions where possible, and mutual co-operation in intervention.

d. *Labour markets*

The feasibility and durability of trade reforms (and the extent to which they and other policy reforms contribute to growth) will also depend critically on the speed of adjustment. That in turn, is closely linked to conditions in labour markets and the speed with which private investment responds to new opportunities. If labour markets are poorly functioning, or if labour finds it difficult to move from an import-competing and contracting industry to an export-oriented and expanding industry, the permanent benefits from trade reforms may take longer to materialise. However, studies regarding labour markets in non-OECD countries concluded that in the absence of pervasive government interventions, these markets operated relatively efficiently. The fact that many workers in non-OECD countries are employed in the informal and agricultural sectors means that firms in expanding sectors can draw on these resources more readily. Nevertheless, worker training and worker assistance programmes can be an important tool in facilitating the transition of workers from employment in sectors that suffer from trade liberalisation to those that benefit.

e. Financial depth

Crafts' (2000) masterly survey of the causes of twentieth century economic growth also sees *financial depth* as a major consideration. He argues that caution in externally liberalising the financial sector is required, but that high priority should be given to developing domestic institutions to ensure honest and effective financial intermediation.

f. Macro-economic management

Another dimension of openness and policy concerns inflation. Romer (1993) suggests that because real depreciation is more costly in open economies, such economies will be more careful to avoid it. That in turn makes them less likely to run the risks of excessive money creation and inflation. He finds that inflation is, indeed, lower for open economies. Fernandez and Portes (1998) make a similar point in discussing the arguments that regional integration arrangements might be used as a means to lock-in better policy regimes. If true, this popular argument could also explain a positive relationship between openness and policy rectitude. Again, the experience of Chile — in this case via compensatory exchange rate policy (see Box 3.1) — is illustrative of macro-economic management as a concomitant to trade policy reform.

D. Are there trade-offs?

The list of possible policies that may accompany trade liberalisation is formidable, but that does not necessarily imply that there are difficult trade-offs (see Box 3.6 for an illustration in the area of services liberalisation). At a technical level, many of the policies are essentially orthogonal in their effects and so require no trading off at all. This *may* not be true of concerns over income distribution, although for every country where openness worsens distribution, there is one for which it improves it. If countries fear this kind of problem as they liberalise, the solution is not to stop liberalising, but to institute compensatory or complementary policies to address them.

Box 3.6. Confronting the complexities of services reform

Pursuit of reform in services is no easy task as it requires balancing the need for regulation to offset market failures with the need to increase the contestability of markets by allowing entry to occur. The gains from reform will be reduced and may not materialise at all if only a subset of the policies that restrict competition are addressed. Examples abound of reform attempts that did not give rise to the expected benefits because other measures remained in place that allowed firms to collude or prevent vigorous competition to emerge.

In addition to a comprehensive approach to reform that considers the broad set of all relevant policies, reforms are complicated by the legitimate role that exists for government to intervene to offset market failures and to achieve non-economic objectives, such as the universal provision of education or health care services. Care must be taken that regulatory reforms are designed so that such objectives continue to be attained in an efficient manner. The case for liberalisation needs to be distinguished from the need for regulation or regulatory reform. Regulation to achieve fiduciary, public health and safety or environmental objectives should be in place and strengthened where necessary, and should apply equally to domestic and foreign service providers.

Liberalisation of the service sector is not a panacea, however, and many of the benefits flowing from greater market openness may take time to materialise. In contrast, the costs associated with the rationalisation of service industries will appear early on under the guise of changes in the structure of industry ownership and possibly labour displacement. Opposition from affected incumbent firms (domestic or foreign) and bureaucracies, who will often perceive liberalisation as a threat to rent-seeking behaviour, add to the complexity of liberalisation efforts with respect to services.

Box 3.6. Confronting the complexities of services reform (cont.)

As with trade in goods, opening cross-border market access in services exposes countries to the potential loss of output and employment. However, it also exposes the domestic economy to greater levels of competition, a larger variety of technologies and products, and a broader market for exploiting scale economies. These benefits to downstream users and final consumers may well offset any losses in the competing service sector.

An important dimension of services trade and investment liberalisation is that the adjustment associated with greater market openness is generally smoother in many service sectors than in some more traditionalareas of goods production. This is so for two reasons, First, adjustment in service industries such as telecommunications and finance often occurs within a dynamic sectoral environment, where expanding market segments and firms can more readily absorb workers from shrinking sectors. Second, owing to a lower degree of sector-specific professional specialisation, service sector employees tend to display greater overall labour market mobility.

Adoption of pro-competitive regulatory reforms and liberalisation of services trade and investment can be expected to help relieve some of the constraints weighing on non-OECD countries' growth potential. Evidence shows that such effects are likely to be greatest with regard to establishment-related trade. Foreign capital inflows provide a higher savings rate and so the potential for a higher investment rate as domestic funds can be diverted to other opportunities. Inflows of foreign capital also lower the balance of payments constraint on growth and allow for lower real interest rates. This, and the boost to short-term growth rates, tends to crowd-in greater domestic investment. As foreign entrants will employ significant numbers of locally hired workers, this process typically sustains the development of human capital and knowledge-based industries.

A trade-off between trade liberalisation and other objectives may also arise in the short run if massive shocks lead to the complete collapse of a market. For example, local labour markets can seize up in the face of large-scale redundancies because natural mobility evaporates: incumbents cease to leave their jobs speculatively because they fear that they will not find another. This is essentially a matter of timing – perhaps of staggering liberalisation, or ensuring that it does not coincide with a negative macro shock.

Similarly, if trade liberalisation leads to the replacement of an official export marketing monopoly by a private one, parts of the sector concerned might cease to be served at all (Winters, 2000). This is essentially a question of the quality of the trade liberalisation. Effective liberalisation does not merely entail removing tariffs or non-tariff barriers, but also requires proper attention to what replaces them. Private monopolies have to be spectacularly more efficient technically before they represent a better solution to economic problems than public ones.

The real trade-offs are political and they come in several forms. First, reform requires support – even for the most repressive of dictators. Edwards and Lederman (1999) document how Chilean firms were compensated for trade reform by labour market reforms that reduced their costs. Moreover, this is not just a matter of sordid log-rolling; rather it resides in what Corden (1984) calls the "Hicksian optimism," that although any single efficiency-enhancing reform will hurt someone, if you package enough of them together, their negative effects will be netted out and nearly everyone will win.

Closely related to this is the effect of uncertainty. Fernandez and Rodrik (1991) have shown that partial uncertainty about who the winners are can lead even risk-neutral societies to reject reforms that they know to be beneficial overall. The "partial" here refers to the assumption that some winners know who they are, but that among the remaining (uncertain) population, the expected value is a loss even though there will be enough winners among them to make up a national majority of winners. In this case, broadening the reform increases the certainty and can actually make it more likely to succeed. If society is risk averse, however, this same effect will be offset by a general reluctance to move into uncertainty.

Societies can demonstrate reform fatigue whereby they become resentful of too much, or too long a period of, change. In this case, timing is necessary to fix priorities. A major problem in this case is maintaining credibility. It is probably better to announce the whole package at the beginning, but ensure that not everyone has to change at once. Then, governments need to recruit the early movers into the coalition to keep the later ones moving.

A similar issue is politician/bureaucratic fatigue. If reform requires constant monitoring or constant selling, a finite bureaucracy or body-politic can only do so much. Diffusion across too many objectives is a well-known cause of failure both in business and in politics, and this issue may well be a binding constraint in many countries. One implication of it is to seek reforms that are simple to do and to maintain. In this regard, a uniform tariff has huge attractions: it is simple to administer and simple to defend from interest groups, and thus takes up very little official time to maintain.

The major area in which these constraints bind is in the various institutional reforms suggested above. Institutions take time to design technically, and given the importance of building up their legitimacy and ownership among the population, they also require a good deal of political time. Moreover, no one gets institutions right first time: they require continuing monitoring and adjustment. As noted above, there are often advantages to proceeding on a broad front, in order to maintain some semblance of fairness, so these institutional reforms are likely to require a long time and considerable official skill to achieve.

E. Trade and growth: summary - the self-healing economy

It is a fact of life that there are nasty surprises. Just as a successful organism is one that can cope with adversity and ultimately adjust, so a successful economy – one with sustained growth - must be able to cope with adverse shocks. This has two implications for our current discussion. First, while policy must display clear focus and vision and must be time-consistent, the precise details, timing and implementation can not be laid down at the very beginning of a reform. Second, flexibility is commonly one of the direct advantages of openness: the economy receives signals about relative values and, by relying on the market, empowers many actors rather than just a few to devise responses to them.

(i) Pragmatism

The implementation of reform calls for pragmatism in addressing the political strains that it inevitably generates. This requires realistic planning and effective treatment of unforeseen sources of opposition, often by accommodation rather than confrontation. The latter is illustrated by the temporary reversal of the Chilean reform in the face of the macroeconomic and terms of trade crisis of 1982: the authorities both increased tariffs in general to raise revenue and offer protection and introduced price bands for wheat, sugar and other commodities to assuage producer groups which had been envisaged as natural allies in reform but which had actually suffered considerably and become very hostile (Edwards and Lederman, 1999).

Rodrik's (1998) emphasis on political institutions for conflict resolution is in the same class as the previous paragraph, but on a larger scale and a longer time horizon. In the long run a reform programme must survive several governments and this will only be possible if it commands legitimacy among at least a significant minority of the population and economic actors. One route to this is if the inevitable surprises are handled by democratic and legitimate institutions, so that losers are unwilling (or unable) to undermine the whole reform process in seeking redress. Arguably legitimising reform will be easier if these institutions are reasonably balanced and equitable in their power structures and the outcomes they engender, and if they are reasonably stable, because, then, parties will be more willing to accept short-term hardship in the expectation of longer-term reward.

A third and equally important aspect of self-healing is to recognise the trial and error component of making economic policy. Again, while theory and experience can lay down broad rules and comparisons with others and can start to identify elements of best practice, every economy and period of time has its own idiosyncrasies. Thus successful policy making requires attention to appraisal and feedback, to ensure that policy is having the desired effects, and the ability to adjust things that are seen not to be working. Amsden (1989) and Wade (1989) both identify such pragmatism as important parts of the success of Korea and Taiwan respectively – noting, for example, the speed with which the former backed away from its heavy industry programme at the end of the 1970s.

(ii) Openness and flexibility

Even the closest managers of an economy cannot consider every detail, whereas, as Adam Smith noted, a community of individuals each responding to self-interest informed by market signals can more or less do so. Governments cannot prevent individuals from making the best of their own particular circumstances (as behaviour under, say, the Soviet system demonstrated), so the key to success is to harness this huge motive force to the right set of signals. This is what market forces do. Subject to the correction of obvious market failures such as missing markets, externalities and public goods, encouraging economic actors to respond flexibly to the incentives they perceive around them generates both strong responses to obvious signals and an informative variety of responses to less obvious ones. Provided that subsequent selection is efficient (*e.g.* Darwinian survival of the fittest) such natural experimentation is a much more reliable way to develop constructive responses to challenges than is bureaucratic centralism.

a. Technology

In the critical area of responding to technological opportunities, the recent dynamism of the US economy seems to illustrate the case well. To be sure, there will be many casualties and a number of major mistakes, such as second-rate technologies gaining footholds and then surviving and propagating themselves via network externalities, and stock-market bubbles as new technologies are over-valued. Overall, however, experience seems to suggest strongly that competition provides the best and most robust of approaches to the problem of economic advance. But this observation is not a case for simple *laissez-faire*. Innovation requires a host of collective or governmental inputs and support:

- access to new ideas, which in the case of the leader country requires public support for basic science;
- effective property rights for innovators, including the right to enjoy their success free of expropriation and penal taxation;
- lending institutions which are able both to take risks and to clear up the mess when things go wrong (bankruptcy), and

- reliable access to markets to sell the fruits of innovation.

For countries that are not technological leaders, the requirements for innovation and the growth that it engenders are similar to those just listed. However, an important short cut – indeed the indispensable source of progress if you can not reach the frontier yourself – is openness to technology from beyond the border. This may be

- obtained by studying foreign patent applications or basic scientific publications from abroad;
- embodied in imports of goods and services;
- based on the knowledge gained from multinational companies or in knowledge transferred via buyer-seller relationships, often within production networks;
- derived from reverse engineering;
- observed abroad during short or long stays (including especially those originating from the provision of services abroad).

For both frontier and other economies, it is clear that education and skills will be critical components of the growth cocktail. Skills might be imported temporarily but long-run development will need an indigenous source. This will require a good deal of conscious investment, usually by government at lower levels of education, and also an ability to learn and disseminate the lessons to be learned from foreign contacts. Kokko and Blomstrom's observation that technology transfer from multinationals is strongest in the face of competition and open markets rather than in the presence of regulations mandating transfer re-inforces the message that openness is key.

b. Price signals

At a more prosaic, but equally important, level, economies have to respond to changes in the scarcity and relative values of goods within the known set of outputs. An economy will be better able to grow if it can quickly move from activities that are becoming less valuable to those that are becoming more so. As with innovation, there is an important set of facilitating circumstances that encourages such flexibility: for example, simple regulations for entering or exiting an industry, access to capital, and risk spreading mechanisms. But open borders also play a central role.

Once one moves beyond the bounds of almost complete autarky, every economy depends ultimately on the world economy as the arbiter of economic value; goods and services are worth no more and no less than the prices at which they can be obtained from or provided to the world market. Thus an economy that admits relatively undistorted signals about world scarcity and permits actors to respond to them is ultimately likely to do a very much better job of creating and preserving value and wealth than one which does not. Perhaps the most graphic examples come from responses to the oil crises of the 1970s and 1980s. Within OECD, Britain resisted change after the 1973 price hike; for nine to twelve months her income appeared to hold up better than those of other European economies, but the ultimate result was an extended period of stasis and crisis. Similarly, Balassa (1985) showed that, among non-OECD countries, although the more open ones suffered larger shocks as a result of the hike in oil prices, they also showed more rapid, and ultimately less costly, adjustment.

Notes

1 Ahn and Hemmings (2000) provide a detailed review of the empirical evidence between trade and growth in OECD countries. ["Policy Influences on Economic Growth in OECD Countries: An Evaluation of the Evidence," Economic Department Working Papers Number 246, OECD, Paris.]

2 Vamvakidis considers only liberalisations up to 1989 in order to leave enough post-reform data to identify growth effects.

3 They argue that Rodriguez and Rodrik's strictures on the cross–country studies should not undermine one's confidence that openness enhances growth, because that view should never have been based on those studies in the first place.

4 See Limao and Venables (2000) on transport costs and their destructive effect on trade and Radelet and Sachs (1998) on their possible growth effects.

5 Mosley goes on to argue that growth responds positively to higher levels of effective protection (at least in poorer countries). Unfortunately, however, his empirics also seem flawed. Effective protection is significant only when weighted by total factor productivity (TFP) growth, which is clearly likely to be correlated with growth on its own.

6 The World Customs Organisation is also critical of PSI because of the costs, the conflicts of interest among PSI companies and the fact that it is an obstacle to customs reform and modernisation. UNCTAD also shares that view. In fact, UNCTAD Recommendation 12 (1994 UN Columbus Ministerial Declaration on Trade Efficiency) states: "*avoiding as far as possible the need to use the services of pre-shipment inspection agencies to carry out customs related activities.*"

7 In no country are consumers well enough organised or possessing sufficient standing to lobby effectively for tariff cuts. Just occasionally, the politics of protection burst out into the sunlight and politicians have to recognise consumer interests. The most prominent example was possibly the renewal of the USA's VER on auto imports from Japan in the mid 1980s, when the co-incidence of an election, record profits for domestic producers and well publicised research showing the huge cost to consumers combined to scupper further protection.

IV. NON-OECD COUNTRIES AND THE STRENGTHENING OF THE MULTILATERAL TRADING SYSTEM

The multilateral trading system (MTS) assists non-OECD countries in their efforts to integrate into the global economy through two inter-connected channels. First, the system supports the process of economic reforms that facilitate the integration of their domestic industries into global production networks. And, second, it seeks to ensure the openness of markets to products of export interest to them.

At the most fundamental level, the WTO defines a framework for the mediation of international trade relations, such that conflicts about trade can be avoided and trade can take place in a stable and predictable environment. The WTO, and its predecessor the GATT, was designed to offer opportunities for mutually beneficial cooperation among nations, where the alternative was mutually destructive defensive behaviour. The WTO can also be seen as a mechanism for mediating domestic conflicts between interest groups. International obligations allow governments to avoid a partisan posture on domestic issues or decisions that make for good politics but bad economics. Thus, for both external and internal reasons, the WTO is intended as a system of rules. These are negotiated by member governments and written into legally binding agreements and shared with the general public so that every concerned party can operate under transparent and predictable trading rules with a consequence of lowering transaction costs.

The dispute settlement function of the WTO supplements its rule-setting role by emphasising the willingness of governments to abide by the defined disciplines. It seeks to ensure that all trade conflicts are resolved harmoniously within the agreed rules which provides added security and certainty to all those engaged in international trade. Simultaneously, the reinforced character of the dispute settlement system has led parties increasingly to seek mutually agreed solutions to their disputes, thus offering an additional, less costly avenue for smaller countries to assert their position.

The significant strengthening of the rules-based system -- through the provision of clear procedural steps towards resolution, the binding nature of decisions, the strengthening of mechanisms for surveillance and enforcement of rulings and the availability of significant sanctions -- has increased the opportunities for smaller trading nations to have a fair hearing and ultimately have their interests upheld. In particular, the possibility for the defendant to block the establishment of a panel and to veto the adoption of a ruling is no longer available. In addition, the newly created option to appeal on a point of law brings additional legal certainty and predictability to the multilateral trading system and the progressive construction of relevant jurisprudence makes the system more accessible to those countries lacking adequate resources and expertise.

Since the dispute settlement understanding came into effect in January 1995 the number of cases has increased significantly as compared to the practice under the GATT 1947. Even under the new rules, the fact of winning a case, especially against a major trading partner, does not necessarily guarantee compliance with a ruling. Compliance largely depends on a defendant's interest in staying within the system and abiding by its rules, so as to be able to benefit from it on other occasions. If retaliation proves necessary, a small trading nation may face the risk that its retaliation has little impact on the defendant. If the economy of the small trading nation is dependent on trade with the larger trading partner, remedial action by the former will likely end up being to its own detriment. Thus, non-OECD countries have a very high stake in further strengthening the dispute settlement system in ways that increasingly dissociate it from the relative economic power of the countries concerned.

In sum, an effective, rules-based multilateral trading system serves the interests of non-OECD countries by providing transparent, credible, predictable and enforceable international trade rules, all of which are necessary elements for a stable and flourishing international economic environment.

The GATT/WTO also sponsors concerted multilateral negotiations that aim to further liberalise the flow of goods and services internationally. Two important benefits emerge from this: (1) there is the enhanced prospect for political acceptability when reform of domestic protection is part of a global effort, or in other words, concerted multilateral liberalisation helps to turn exporters into a more coherent force for import liberalisation; and (2) there is the additional benefit that can accrue from liberalisation by others; that is, the gains from trade liberalisation tend to be greater the larger the number of countries involved.

This is not to say that trade liberalisation can be made into a welfare gain only if reciprocated.[1] Such a mercantilist motivation finds little support in economic reasoning. However, political arguments lend support to this approach. In a democratic society, it is easier to secure trade liberalisation over the opposition of affected domestic producers if a government can show that additional market openings will result from its own trade liberalisation actions. Reciprocal bargaining on trade liberalisation may be able to secure more open markets than the economically rational course of unilateral trade liberalisation.

It is clear from the above that for non-OECD countries, be they small, medium-sized or even large economies, trading in the international markets on the basis of strong and enforceable rules and disciplines agreed through multilateral, rather than bilateral negotiations is of critical importance to them. In fact, the case can be made that the WTO system is relatively more important to non-OECD countries than for OECD countries. There are at least two reasons why this is the case. First, some OECD countries have enough bargaining power to unilaterally influence the behaviour of others. And, second, non-OECD countries have a larger stake in a healthy growing world economy. In other words, the more rules are developed at the multilateral level and the more disputes resolved at that level, the more likely that the trading interests of non-OECD countries will be protected. It is thus not surprising to see that the most important accomplishments of the Uruguay Round in as far as non-OECD countries are concerned were the substantial strengthening of the rules governing the conduct of international trade and their extension to new areas of activities, and the protection of all of these through an efficient and effective dispute settlement procedure.

In addition to sharing a common interest in the strength of the multilateral trading system, all non-OECD countries, be they importers or exporters of this or that product or service, look to the system to further their own trading needs. These include, *inter alia*, ensuring the timely and full implementation of all Uruguay Round Agreements, including those of interest to them (*e.g.* in such sectors as textiles and clothing, and agriculture; and in areas such as special and differential treatment, technical assistance and problems of the least developed countries). Non-OECD countries also want the system to develop in a manner that will continue to serve their interests, be that in the area of existing rules (*e.g.* anti-dumping, countervailing duties, safeguards, and technical barriers to trade), contemplated rules (*e.g.* in respect of trade and environment), and promoting further liberalisation in areas of export interest to them (*e.g.* further reductions in goods tariffs and liberalisation of agriculture and services activities).

A. Market access in goods

The massive reductions in tariffs, and the establishment of the principle that non-discriminatory tariffs are the principal means of trade protection are commonly viewed as one of the most significant success stories of post-war trade policy and multilateral trade negotiations under the GATT. The Uruguay Round marked the eighth time that GATT Contracting Parties have negotiated reductions of trade barriers in a multilateral framework. The success of these multilateral trade negotiations (MTNs) has been remarkable. Prior to the Uruguay Round, seven Rounds of MTNs had succeeded in lowering the average (trade-weighted) most-favoured-nation (MFN) tariff rates on industrial goods from a high of 40 per cent at the end of World War II to around 6 per cent at the end of the Tokyo Round (1974-79). And the Uruguay Round (1986-93) further reduced the average trade-weighted tariff rates to 4 per cent.

Nevertheless, market access still represents perhaps the single most important trading issue between OECD and non-OECD countries. Non-OECD countries' strongest demands are not only for continued access to OECD countries' markets, but also for increased access. On the other hand, OECD countries look for non-OECD governments to participate more effectively in multilateral negotiations, and for some of them to contribute more to liberalisation and rule-making efforts and to assume more GATT/WTO obligations. In other words, some non-OECD countries should "graduate" from the status of "developing country" that confers special treatment under the rules, and preferential access to major OECD markets. For both groups of countries, market access has been hindered by many barriers: tariffs and non-tariffs barriers, contingency protection measures, and indeterminate measures such as voluntary export restraints (VERs).

As will be described below, completion of the Uruguay Round of trade negotiations has resulted in broad based tariff reductions and the easing of some of the most important non-tariff barriers, strongly enhancing the prospects for reaping global welfare gains from further trade expansion.

(i) Tariffs

The continuing reductions of tariffs suggest that progress toward trade liberalisation has been steady and marked. It would also seem that the process has occurred reciprocally among most trading nations. However, several reservations can be registered about this picture.

Table 4.1 shows that tariff reductions offered by OECD countries on imports from their non-OECD partners (30%) were lower than those granted to other OECD countries (45%). Thus, the mean trade-weighted tariff in OECD countries on imports from other OECD origins stands at 3%, as opposed to 4.8% on imports from non-OECD countries.

Simultaneously, non-OECD countries' tariff reductions on imports from OECD countries (28%) were lower than those offered by OECD countries to imports from other non-OECD countries (30%) Moreover, average tariffs in non-OECD countries remain higher in absolute terms than those that prevail in OECD countries, and are relatively higher on imports from OECD countries than on those that originate from other non-OECD countries. Trade-weighted tariffs in non-OECD countries on imports from OECD are now 10.7%, more than double OECD's own tariffs against imports from non-OECD countries (4.8%).

Thus it appears that progress towards tariff liberalisation has not proceeded at the same speed across countries; nor has it achieved the same depth throughout. The fact that non-OECD countries did not fully participate in the tariff negotiations processes prior to the Uruguay Round provides one explanation why the results so far reflect less than an optimal solution.

The same can be said in respect of tariff reduction achievements across major product groups. With regard to imports of industrial products, OECD trade-weighted mean tariffs on imports from non-OECD countries vary from a low of 1% on imports of metals to a high of 12% placed against imports of textiles and clothing products. Such a margin points to the presence of some tariff peaks, an observation that is confirmed by inspecting the data reported in Table 4.2 where OECD countries' tariff profiles by major industrial group are shown. For example, some 28% of textile and clothing imports enter OECD markets at duties in excess of 15%. A similar pattern can also be observed in respect of imports of leather, rubber, footwear and travel goods. All these are product groups in which non-OECD countries enjoy a comparative advantage

It is thus clear that although the situation has improved considerably following the Uruguay Round, tariff reductions have not been even for all products. It is also the case that tariff reductions have not been even across broad sectors. This is most obvious in the case of agricultural imports where it was agreed to convert all border measures such as quotas and variable levies into tariffs (tariffication). In some cases, the tariffication process involved the introduction of tariff rate quotas at high levels. Food products with high tariffs in OECD countries include (1) major agricultural food products, such as meat, sugar, milk, dairy products, and chocolate, where tariff rates frequently exceed 100 per cent; (2) tobacco and some alcoholic beverages; (3) fruits and vegetables—including 180 per cent for above-quota bananas in the European Union and 550 per cent and 132% for shelled groundnuts in Japan and the United States, respectively; (4) food industry products, including fruit juices, canned meat, peanut butter, and sugar confectionery, with rates exceeding 30% in several markets. Again, all these are products in which non-OECD countries enjoy a comparative advantage.

Although the Uruguay Round has managed to reduce the trade bias originating from the practice of tariff escalation, it has not eliminated it. Tariffs increase from raw to finished products: the average post-Uruguay Round tariff for all industrial products goes from 0.8% on raw materials to 4.8% on the finished product (Table 4.3). Therefore, further progress on this front should offer gains for a number of non-OECD countries.

In the pre-Uruguay Round trading environment, MFN tariffs in many sectors were not legally bound, and as such could be raised easily. This created a lack of security in market access, and may have produced detrimental trade effects. A major goal of the Round has been to increase the proportion of industrial tariffs that are bound, thus providing added protection to trade liberalisation commitments. This goal has been successfully met: the percentage of OECD countries' imports of industrial goods under bound duties rose from 94% to 99%. In the non-OECD area, countries in Latin America were the greatest achievers, as the totality of their industrial tariff lines were bound. Asia remains the region least committed to binding its tariffs on industrial goods: only 67%of its tariff lines covering 70% of industrial imports are now bound.

In the area of agriculture, comprehensive information on the levels of bindings by major country group is not available. However, a recent study by the OECD (OECD, 1999) found that on average, OECD countries bound close to 99% of their agricultural tariff lines, an achievement which is similar to that in a sample of thirteen non-OECD countries.

What the above observations mean in practice is that there remains ample scope for benefits to accrue from multilateral tariff liberalisation. A full development of trade links between OECD and non-OECD countries requires progress in dismantling remaining tariff restrictions on certain sensitive industrial products and agriculture, more often product categories where many non-OECD countries enjoy a comparative advantage.

(ii) Non-tariff barriers

By contrast to tariffs, non-tariff barriers have continued to be a more complicated issue for policymakers and policy analysts. To put it simply, less is known about non-tariff barriers. Reliable information identifying non-tariff barriers and assessing their role in market access within and across countries is not readily available. Therefore, before discussing the Uruguay Round results with respect to non-tariff barriers, it is worth briefly outlining what is known.

a. Non-tariff barriers and the relative openness of markets

Several rankings of the overall relative competitiveness or openness of import markets exist (*e.g.*, Sachs and Warner 1999). The data show that the degree of market openness tends to be positively related to per capita GDP. Sachs and Warner find this relationship specifically between business perceptions of hidden import barriers and per capita GDP (Figure 4.1).[2] The greater the impact of non-tariff barriers on market access, the higher the economic cost to the importing country.

Figure 4.1. **GDP and executives' perceptions about hidden import barriers**

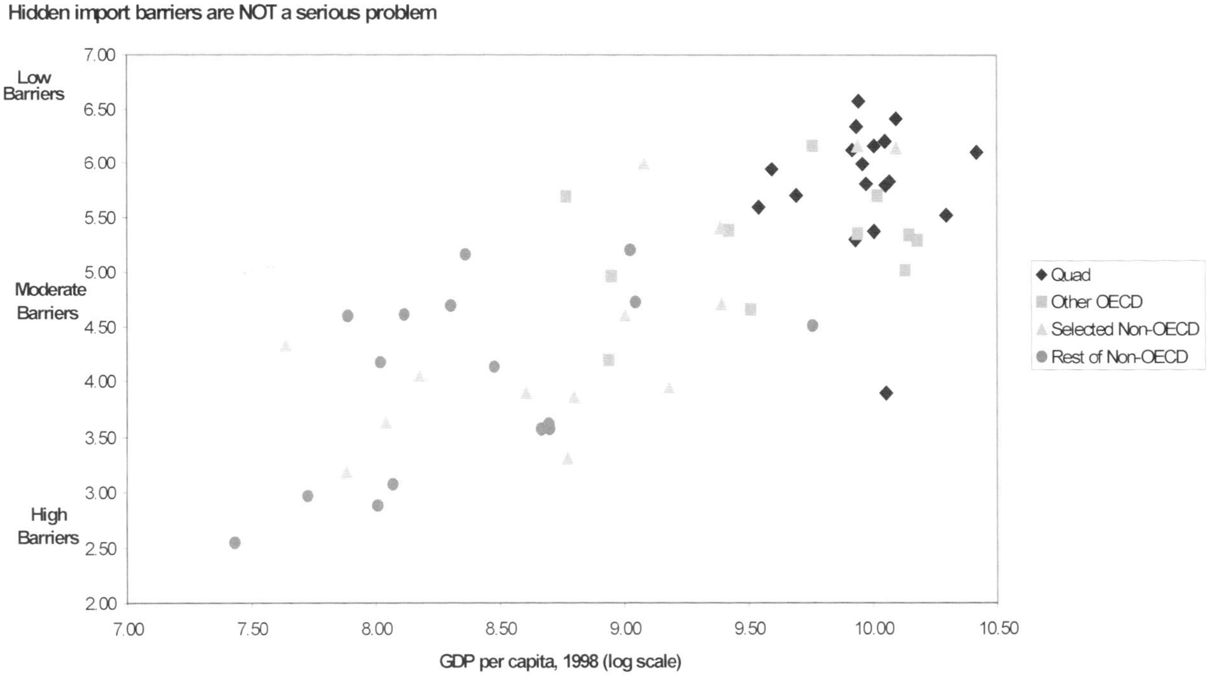

1. Figure notes: For the purpose of this chart, selected non-OECD countries consist of China; Russia; India; Brazil; Argentina; Slovak Republic; Hong Kong, China; Singapore; Chile; Indonesia; Philippines; Malaysia; Chinese Taipei and Thailand. The rest of non-OECD countries comprise Colombia, Egypt, Israel, Jordan, Peru, South Africa, Vietnam, Venezuela, Costa Rica, El Salvador, Ukraine, Bulgaria, Zimbabwe, Bolivia, Ecuador and Mauritius.
2. GDP per capita is shown as a scale of natural logarithms; data range from 7.43 = $1 689 to 10.42 = $33 505.

Source: OECD Secretariat, based on J.D. Sachs and A.M. Warner 'A Year in Review (1999)', Global Competitiveness Report. The hidden barriers data were taken from the 1999 World Economic Forum survey of 3,934 senior business leaders and government officials in 58 countries, of which 26% from domestic companies, 42% from significant exporters, 25% from multinationals operating in the country, and 7% from government.

b. *Non-tariff barriers -- what they are and where they are*

While these types of broad analyses exist, less is known about the specific constitution of barriers either across countries or within individual sectors or product categories, particularly outside of agriculture and related products. And even less is known about the relative importance of market access problems within and across countries.

Most current sources of data only reflect the reported frequency of non-tariff measures for certain sectors and countries. The frequency of barriers does not equate with the degree of market closure. For example, a single import-licensing requirement may effectively close a market but counts as only one barrier in a frequency analysis. By contrast, another market may have large imports even where a frequency analysis shows several technical or other requirements. Also, for many countries, little information on their trade practices is publicly available or reported. Therefore, frequencies of reported barriers are likely to misrepresent their relative impact on and across markets.

The concerns about non-tariff barriers have changed over time, with an increase in the apparent importance of non-border measures. These can take the form of behind-the-border policies (such as entry restrictions into a foreign distribution system). Or they may be procedural barriers related to policy implementation that have not been adequately accounted for in extant data (such as problems related to arbitrariness or a lack of transparency in importing-country procedures). However, there is no commonly agreed-upon definition of what policies and practices should be covered in any analysis of non-tariff barriers. In certain cases, what one exporter calls a trade barrier may be a necessary or legitimate policy or practice by the importing country.

To date, attempts to improve the available information have been limited, as have been the concomitant results. The OECD has initiated some work in this area.. In particular, the OECD is attempting to develop a generic typology of non-tariff barriers in goods that better reflects current realities.

c. *Non-tariff barriers and the Uruguay Round market access commitments*

In the non-tariff field, a major achievement of the Uruguay Round was agreement on liberalisation in several important areas of the world economy and the strengthening of the rules and disciplines governing the conduct of international trade. However, by their very nature, some of the liberalisation and rule-making achievements will bring dividends mainly in a gradual manner. As such, they necessarily depend on further efforts to implement and deepen the commitments in a multilateral context. The efforts accomplished and anticipated should strongly benefit all countries, in particular non-OECD countries, who feel that their interests have often not been fully addressed by the multilateral trading system in the past.

The areas of liberalisation agreed in the Uruguay Round of major interest to non-OECD countries included especially the reform of the textiles and clothing and the agriculture sectors (see Box 4.1). The abolition of voluntary export restraints (VERs) was also of particular interest for strengthening the ability of manufacturers in many countries to compete internationally. Nonetheless, and as was pointed out in the previous section, there remain significant tariff barriers in OECD markets on imports of textiles, clothing and agricultural products originating from non-OECD countries. These are product groups where non-OECD countries have a comparative advantage.

In addition, non-OECD countries have expressed concerns over the product integration process in the Agreement on Textiles and Clothing (ATC). They point out that, overall, products integrated thus far into the WTO have been concentrated in the relatively low value-added range, and the phase-out process has been "back-loaded," in the sense that almost half of the quantitative restrictions (those shielding the most sensitive items) will be removed at the end of the transition period. Some non-OECD countries also fear that back-loaded liberalisation will distort the distribution of benefits amongst them. In any case, these countries have expressed the view that even following the full phase-out of all MFA-related quotas, continued application of relatively high tariff barriers will remain of concern. These concerns are in fact being addressed in the WTO.

In the area of agriculture, some non-OECD countries have expressed concerns that under-filled quotas combined with high out-of-quota tariffs have led to trade distortions. Issues related to implementation have also raised concerns in some non-OECD countries. In particular, the use of other policies that may have subsidy elements, including export credits, the activities of state trading entities as well as export taxes and restraints on exports have attracted increasing attention. Net food importing developing countries may also see a rise in their food import bill to the extent that some concessional arrangements are being eliminated or because of a rise in world agricultural prices. Despite these concerns, the URAA represents a major step toward the establishment of a set of multilateral rules for agricultural trade.

In addition, progress has been registered in ensuring that technical regulations and standards do not become trade barriers. The Agreements on Technical Barriers to Trade (TBT) and on Sanitary and Phytosanitary Measures (SPS) define rules for the preparation, adoption and application of technical regulations and standards, including in the area of sanitary and phytosanitary protection and covering a wide range of product quality and safety issues. The major goals are to ensure that such measures are not more trade-restrictive than necessary to achieve legitimate national objectives and that like products receive non-discriminatory treatment. These rules help open world-wide markets to exports from producers that conform to internationally recognised standards. A challenge faced by non-OECD countries is thus to adapt their exports to such standards. Rising consumer concerns in developed countries over food quality and safety compound the difficulties that many non-OECD countries experience in this regard. At the same time, there is a need for non-OECD countries to become more involved in the setting of international standards and technical regulations.

Progress on NTBs -- as on all trade barriers -- is a priority for non-OECD countries for a number of reasons. First, these typically small economies are reliant on industrial-country markets to drive their own economic growth. Second, non-OECD countries generally have comparative advantages in a much smaller range of goods than do large developed countries. Consequently, NTBs limiting market access for these goods have a pronounced negative effect on countries' economic growth potential. Since NTBs are less transparent than tariffs and are notoriously difficult to identify and measure, they often offer more room for discretionary action by governments and create uncertainty, thus discouraging investment and trade and slowing development.

It has been estimated that once the Uruguay Round is fully implemented, the share of imports from non-OECD countries affected by OECD countries' non-tariff barriers (including the MFA) will drop from around 18% to 4.2-5.5%.[3] Although these figures do not reflect the restrictiveness of measures, nor do they include the broader universe of more recently perceived NTBs (such as procedural barriers), this reduction will create significant export opportunities for non-OECD countries. Actually achieving this degree of liberalisation -- through implementation of commitments and undertaking of new ones -- will remain a strong challenge for the future.

With the progressive reduction in tariffs and non-tariff barriers, further promotion of competition depends critically on the reform of "behind-the-border" barriers - notably, domestic regulation, restrictions on service sector activities, government procurement and subsidies. Along with progress on the traditional agenda of tariffs and NTBs, the Uruguay Round built up momentum to tackle these issues - witness the signing of three new agreements: the General Agreement on Trade in Services (GATS), the Agreement on Trade-related Aspects of Intellectual Property Rights (TRIPS) and the Agreement on the Application of Sanitary and Phytosanitary Measures (SPS), plus the reform of the Agreement on Technical Barriers to Trade (TBT).

Box 4.1. Progress in two critical sectors for non-OECD countries.

The Uruguay Round Agreements on Textiles and Clothing (ATC) and on Agriculture (URAA) have put an end to exemptions from basic GATT principles and disciplines that these sectors received for decades. The ATC provides for the gradual elimination by 2005 of the special regime of country-specific quantitative restrictions for trade in textiles and clothing that was GATT-legitimised with the "Multi-Fibre Arrangement" (MFA) in the mid-1970s. The URAA establishes a rules-based trading system for agricultural products for all WTO members by subjecting three major policy domains (market access, domestic support and export competition) to specific WTO disciplines and reduction commitments.

Textiles and Clothing

Textiles and clothing are an area of special importance for non-OECD countries. In the early 1990s the sector represented 22% of non-OECD countries' export earnings from industrial products -- the most significant category of such products.[4]

Forty years of managed trade in textiles and clothing have perpetuated significant trade and production distortions and have simultaneously created strong vested interests opposed to a rapid phasing out of MFA restrictions. The ATC represents a collective agreement to put an end to the MFA regime, through progressive abolition of quantitative restrictions on the basis of a multi-factor formula to be implemented over a period of ten years, ending with complete quota elimination on 31 December 2004.

The ATC is facilitating increased exports of textiles and clothing products from non-OECD countries, which are encountering fewer and less stringent quantitative restrictions in their major import markets. Although implementation has been subject to some controversy, the Agreement has so far been applied consistently with its legal provisions, and two MFA countries (Canada and Norway) have unilaterally carried out advanced integration measures beyond those required by the ATC -- Norway has already eliminated virtually all its quotas.

Non-OECD countries are expected to be the key beneficiaries of the ATC. According to some estimates, world trade in textiles and apparel may increase by as much as 34-60% once the MFA phase-out is completed.[5] The WTO Secretariat has estimated that exports of textiles and clothing from non-OECD countries to OECD countries could increase by more than 80% over the phase-out period of the MFA.

Notwithstanding the very significant achievement represented by the ATC, concerns have been expressed, particularly by non-OECD countries, regarding the benefits they have so far received from the progressive implementation of the Agreement. These countries point out that, overall, products integrated into the WTO thus far have been concentrated in the relatively low value-added range and the phase-out process has been "back-loaded" in the sense that almost half of the quantitative restrictions – those shielding the most sensitive items – will be removed only at the end of the transition period. While non-OECD-country exporters are concerned that OECD Governments will have difficulty overcoming industry objections to liberalisation, OECD signatories have continually stressed their full commitment to the ATC.

In addition, some non-OECD countries fear that back-loaded liberalisation will distort the distribution of benefits among non-OECD countries at a time when rapid structural change will be necessary. They are concerned that the MFA has created entrenched export interests protected from open competition, particularly from newer and possibly more efficient producers. Consequently, the dismantling of the MFA may entail significant adjustment costs for some non-OECD countries that have been major exporters under the MFA.

Box 4.1. Progress in two critical sectors for non-OECD countries. (cont.)

Furthermore, some countries feel that further distortions have been introduced by the preferential access accorded to some non-OECD countries to selected OECD markets, as through the Europe Agreements. As a result, these countries enjoy better market access than other competitors from non-OECD countries, some of whom may be lower-cost exporters. Clearly, continued application of relatively high tariff barriers will remain a cause of concern, even after all MFA-related quotas have been abolished.

These concerns have been raised and are being addressed in the WTO. In addition to bringing the textiles and clothing sector into the mainstream of GATT rules, the WTO provides a system, the Textile Monitoring Body, to oversee the implementation of the Agreement, as well as a forum to deal with controversies and problems that may arise. Moreover, the strengthened dispute settlement system established by the broader Uruguay Round Agreements provides an effective mechanism to deal with potential violations of WTO commitments.

Agriculture

The agricultural sector plays an important role in the economies of a large number of non-OECD countries. In 1998, agriculture accounted for 12% of total GDP of middle income non-OECD countries and it represented 11% of total merchandise exports. These numbers rise considerably for the Least Developed Countries.[6]

The URAA marked a historic point in the reform of the agricultural trading system. The Agreement has brought systemic changes in the way agricultural policymakers are addressing agricultural issues. Specifically, for "developing countries," (reference to developing countries here follows WTO practice) the URAA provides for differentiated treatment through specific exemptions from reduction commitments and extended deadlines for implementation. At the same time, concerns have been expressed, regarding perceived weaknesses of certain specific features of the Agreement.

On market access commitments, the replacement of non-tariff measures by tariff equivalents ("tariffication") has resulted in the elimination of highly discretionary and distorting policy instruments. Even though in most OECD countries average agricultural tariffs are higher than non-agricultural tariffs, the URAA provides for greater transparency in protection and a clear starting point for future tariff reduction negotiations. Moreover, the provisions for "market access opportunities" have led to the introduction of tariff-quotas that in some cases have opened up markets formerly closed or restricted. At the same time, there have been concerns that under-filled quotas combined with high out-of-quota tariffs have resulted in trade distortions. Even though there are several factors that can lead to under-utilisation of tariff-quotas, the manner in which tariff-quotas are administered are seen to have an important impact on the rate of fill.

The domestic support provisions represent a major breakthrough, as they explicitly recognise the direct link between domestic agricultural policies and international trade. Nevertheless, their quantitative effects on agricultural trade have so far been modest. This is attributed by some to the aggregate (*i.e.* non-product-specific) nature of the reduction commitments and the exclusion of some support measures, *i.e.* "blue box" (payments under production-limiting programmes) and "green box" payments (domestic support policies that have "little or no" trade impact) that in some cases may not be production and trade neutral.

In comparison, the URAA's disciplines on export subsidies have had a more immediate quantitative impact on agricultural trade. The Agreement imposed strict limits on agricultural export subsidies, and the total amount of export subsidies has been curtailed. Notwithstanding the achievements in this area, some

Box 4.1. Progress in two critical sectors for non-OECD countries. (cont.)

concerns have been expressed regarding implementation issues. In particular, the use of other policies that may have subsidy elements, including export credits, the activities of state trading entities as well as export taxes and restraints on exports, have attracted increasing attention.

The elimination of past production and trade distortions may also involve some costs and risks for net food importing developing countries that so far have been importing a large share of their food consumption at the generally depressed world market prices, and through several concessional arrangements. Concern has been expressed that such countries may now find themselves facing higher food import bills to the extent that some of these concessional arrangements are being eliminated or because of a rise in the level of world agricultural prices.

Despite the concerns outlined here, the URAA represents a major step toward the establishment of a set of multilateral rules for agricultural trade. The requirement to tariffy non-tariff barriers, to quantify the Aggregate Measure of Support, and to notify all subsequent policy changes to the WTO's Committee on Agriculture are major contributions to transparency that in themselves limit the worst excesses. Also, the ability of the strengthened dispute settlement system to deal with trade conflicts is particularly relevant for trade in agricultural products, where disputes are relatively frequent. Furthermore, the Uruguay Round has provided the basis for further WTO negotiations to provide additional progressive reductions in agricultural support and protection. These negotiations are currently underway and non-OECD countries have substantial interests in achieving progress.

B. Liberalisation of services

The agreement to create a General Agreement on Trade in Services (GATS) was one of the major innovations to emerge from the Uruguay Round in 1994. Simply put, as far as trade and investment in services is concerned, the GATS *is* the multilateral system. It offers all the benefits that the GATT has provided for goods trade for more than five decades, the most essential of which is the stability and civility provided by a system of law and the binding nature of commitments on market access and national treatment which WTO member countries assume in their national schedules. Stability makes long-term planning possible, and in service industries where direct investment is often the only way to compete effectively in a market, this is critical. The "signalling" properties of the GATS are particularly important for non-OECD countries. This is especially so for the least developed countries, many of which fail to register adequately on foreign investors' radar screens and consequently carry high and potentially FDI-deterring risk premia.

Governments at all levels of development today recognise the vital role that an efficient and vibrant service industry plays in the process of economic and social development. Unilateral (autonomous) reform efforts are being undertaken by numerous countries. The issue then is how to fit these into the GATS; how to use the GATS to push domestic reform efforts forward; how to respond to pressure by other countries that desire greater access to the domestic market; and what to ask in return.

The multilateral liberalisation of services trade is more difficult to achieve than is the case with merchandise trade, as the characteristics of services and the regulatory nature of measures restricting trade and investment in the sector lend themselves less readily to the method of reciprocal exchange of market access "concessions." The challenge for non-OECD countries is thus to develop negotiation modalities that allow governments to use the GATS as a complementary means of pursuing desired domestic reforms, while improving access to foreign markets.

Precious little liberalisation of trade in services occurred during the Uruguay Round. Instead, a framework was created under which progressive liberalisation could be pursued in the future. For non-OECD countries, the launch of the GATS 2000 round raises the twin questions of what the negotiating agenda should be, and how the multilateral process can best be harnessed to make it more conducive to the realisation of development objectives.

The most obvious GATS deficiency at present lies in the number and quality of liberalisation commitments: the sectoral coverage of many national schedules is small and many of the commitments which do exist are either subject to important limitations or fail even to lock in the regulatory *status quo*. Such deficiencies are most acute in the case of non-OECD countries, though the scope for broadening and deepening the level of trade and investment liberalisation is also significant in the case of OECD countries.

Perhaps the best measure of the state of liberalisation that is embodied in the GATS is the share of commitments where no restrictions are maintained on either market access or national treatment. The figure for high income countries is 25% of all services, for other countries, less than 10% (Hoekman and Mattoo, 1999). These numbers vividly illustrate how far away GATS members are from attaining "free trade" in services, and the magnitude of the task that lies ahead.[7]

One reason for the reluctance of governments in non-OECD countries to lock in reform programmes has been a perceived need to protect incumbent suppliers from immediate competition—either because of infant industry-type of arguments or to facilitate "orderly adjustment." Yet the observed failure of infant industry policies lies to an important degree in the difficulty many governments experience in committing credibly to liberalisation at some future date. This tends to occur either because governments often have a direct stake in the national firm's continued operation, or because they are vulnerable to pressure from interest groups (domestic and foreign) who stand to benefit from continued protection.

To harness the full potential of the GATS, countries should use the opportunity of the current negotiations to aim for a significant expansion in the number and coverage of commitments and for the removal wherever possible of existing limitations.[8] An important start in this regard could be made in the key area of transport, both maritime and air, where little progress proved possible in the first round of GATS negotiations. As former WTO Director-General Renato Ruggiero aptly noted: "It will be hard to claim that the GATS provides the basic infrastructure for world trade so long as the services which carry the world's goods and service providers are not properly covered by it." (Ruggiero, 1998).

The GATS offers a potentially valuable mechanism to overcome the difficulty of making credible promises to liberalise and to promote orderly adjustment by allowing commitments to provide market access and national treatment at a future date. A pre-commitment to liberalise can also instil a sense of urgency to domestic reform, and to speed up efforts to develop necessary regulatory and supervisory mechanisms.[9]

Arguments by economists that the WTO can be used as a valuable credibility-bolstering device have proven less than fully compelling at the negotiating table. In practice, the mercantilist logic of multilateral negotiations suggests that industrialised countries will need to improve export opportunities for non-OECD countries, both within and beyond the services field.

Regardless of the negotiation modalities GATS members agree on (*e.g.* request-offer exchanges and/or formula-based approaches), priority attention should be given to key "backbone" or "enabling" sectors such as transportation, telecommunications, financial services and energy, as well as to clusters of related activities that are vital to economic development and to greater participation in the world economy (*e.g.*, e-commerce, multi-modal transport and express courier services). Increasing the efficiency of such service sectors will have major payoffs for non-OECD countries in terms of lower prices, higher quality, and greater product differentiation.[10]

From a mercantilist perspective, such infrastructural services are sectors where enterprises in industrialised countries can be expected to dominate the supply side. Traditional negotiating balance imperatives therefore suggest that services and modes of supply where non-OECD countries have an export interest also be put on the table. Without such concessions, non-OECD countries are unlikely to use the GATS to bind the *status quo* or as a pre-commitment device for planned future reforms.

Potential tradeoffs within the ambit of the services negotiations can be readily identified (see Box 4.2). For example, non-OECD countries have an interest in seeking commitments in the area of national social and medical insurance regimes, to allow patients to undergo medical treatment abroad. Perhaps the largest potential area for commercially meaningful tradeoffs concerns liberalisation of mode 4 services trade, involving the temporary entry of service providers. Although traditionally a sensitive policy area in many OECD countries, labour mobility is one issue where incremental progress could be made in the new GATS round.[11] It is also an area where opposition within OECD countries is not monolithic - there are indeed many "user" industries that would benefit from - and clamour loudly for - more liberal temporary access regimes, and the development of coalitions with such industries could help change the *status quo*.

Box 4.2. Addressing the service export priorities of non-OECD countries

There are likely to be significant gains world-wide if restrictions on services exports from non-OECD countries are eliminated. With greater liberalisation, particularly in so-called "mode 4" trade, which involves the temporary movement of service suppliers, many more non-OECD countries could "export" at least the significant labour component of services, particularly in industries such as construction, distribution, transportation and environmental services.

Perhaps the most striking recent example of a non-OECD country service export success story is the Indian software industry, which has emerged as a significant supplier to OECD country markets. Indian software exports grew from $225 million in 1992-93 to $2.65 billion in 1998-1999, a compound annual growth rate exceeding 50 percent. The sector accounts for 10.5% of total Indian exports today, up from 2.5 per cent a mere five years ago. It is estimated that two of every five Fortune 500 companies outsourced their software requirements to India last year. In 1999-2000, India exported software-related services to 95 countries. Of the total, 62 per cent of software exports went to North America, and about a quarter to Europe.

Despite the growing importance of cross-border electronic delivery of software services, the movement of natural persons remains a crucial mode of delivery in the sector. Even though the share of on-shore services in total Indian software exports has been in continuous decline (in 1988, the percentage of on-site development stood at nearly 90 per cent), about 60% of Indian exports are still supplied through the temporary movement of programmers. That is, final services are delivered on-shore at the client's site overseas.

In the early 1990s, the US government introduced rules that obliged foreign workers to acquire temporary work visas (H1-B visas), and limited the number of visas issued yearly to 65,000. This contributed to the relative decline of on-shore services by Indian firms (Heeks, 1998). In 1998, in response to mounting labour shortages experienced in the US ICT sector, the annual visa cap was raised to 115,000 for both 1999 and 2000. This quota increase has led to a boost in US on-site imports of software services, especially in the wake of "Y2K" work. Demand for scarce computer skills has remained buoyant in the face of continued growth in IT spending. This has prompted many industry voices throughout the OECD area to seek wider access to foreign talent pools and revisit current immigration and labour market policy restricting entry of highly skilled individuals.

Box 4.2. Addressing the service export priorities of non-OECD countries (cont.)

Significant gains can be had from further liberalisation of mode 4 services trade in the ICT sector. There are wide differences in the cost of software development and support: the average cost per line of software code in Switzerland (the most expensive country in the OECD area) exceeds by more than a factor of five that of India, and the average salaries of computer programmers are more than eleven times higher in Switzerland than in India. Even though differences in labour productivity imply that a lower average salary of programmers may not necessarily translate into a lower average cost per line of software code, by outsourcing programming activities, firms in OECD countries can achieve significant savings in development and support costs. Against the background of a total market for software services worth about $58 billion in the US, $42 billion in Europe and $10 billion in Japan, such cost savings could well be substantial. Other gains from trade liberalisation for importing countries include a more competitive market structure for software services, increased choice, as countries may develop a special expertise for certain development or support services, and a greater diffusion of knowledge. (Mattoo 1999a, Chadha 1999b).

Dealing with domestic regulations

Strengthened multilateral disciplines on domestic regulations can play a significant role in promoting and consolidating domestic regulatory reform. Such disciplines can also equip non-OECD country exporters with the means to address regulatory barriers to their own exports in foreign markets. For example, disciplines to deal with licensing and qualification requirements for professionals are necessary if market access commitments on mode 4 (temporary entry) are to have any value. One of the ironies of the GATS is that the provisions dealing with domestic regulations are among its weakest. This is largely a reflection of the difficulty of developing effective multilateral disciplines in this area without seeming to encroach upon national sovereignty and unduly limiting regulatory freedom.

The need for effective regulation, for instance in the critically important financial sector, requires little elaboration, particularly in light of the recent experiences of many countries. It is incumbent on GATS members themselves to create adequate mechanisms for such regulation, which is clearly necessary if countries are to benefit fully from liberalisation. At the same time, non-OECD countries must be mindful of the fact that the inadequacy of regulatory regimes and institutions can inhibit the export potential of domestic service firms. For instance, in professional services, low standards and disparities in domestic training and examinations can become major impediments to obtaining foreign recognition. Care must thus be taken to avoid instances where inadequacies in domestic regulation can legitimise external barriers to trade.

C. Building Trade Disciplines

As stated above, the Uruguay Round Agreements constitute a rule-writing exercise intended to forestall the protectionist abuse of other types of government interventions (especially domestic policies) and establish a level playing field for, and enhance predictability of national policies.

Agreements which illustrate how emerging global disciplines can contribute to the stability of the international trading system, from which both OECD and non-OECD countries benefit alike, relate, among others, to trade-related investment measures (TRIMs), trade-related intellectual property rights (TRIPs), the use of anti-dumping and countervailing measures and customs valuation procedures:

- The Agreement on TRIMs seeks to discipline the use of certain restrictions or conditions on foreign investment that have a direct influence on trade, provide disincentives to foreign investors, and curtail the quality and choice of competitively priced products available to consumers.[12] This is important for non-OECD countries because the issue of how to attract capital, especially long-term foreign direct investment (FDI), to support faster and sustained growth, is one of the most critical issues facing these countries. The two typical measures that are listed in the Illustrative List that are inconsistent with the TRIMs are domestic content requirements and trade balancing measures, both unjustified on efficiency grounds. Domestic content requirements, often coupled with import restrictions, hinder the capturing of economies of scale and delay the introduction of new technologies. Protection, typically justified by infant industry arguments, results in increased entry to the protected sector, leading further to under-scaled operations and thus efficiency loss. Together with delayed introduction of new technology resulting from "local content requirements," this makes foreign firms push up prices and generate a vicious circle of interventions. Trade balancing requirements limit enterprises in their taping of new sources for inputs, therefore hindering competition and leading to higher costs.

- The Agreement on TRIPs establishes broad international minimum standards of protection, including in the areas of patents, trademarks, copyrights and geographical indicators. It has clear provisions on MFN and national treatment clauses and on transparency. Perhaps the most important benefit of TRIPS to WTO members, including non-OECD countries, is the establishment of multilateral disciplines over IPR conflicts through the dispute settlement process. Protection offers obvious benefits to intellectual property holders, who are mainly based in OECD countries, but there are potential economic gains accruing also to non-OECD countries over the longer run (*e.g.* increased research and development activity, transfer of technology).

- The Uruguay Round clarified the circumstances and procedures for applying certain types of measures, such as anti-dumping duties, subsidies and countervailing duties. In the case of the Anti-dumping Agreement, in order to provide greater clarity and predictability to existing disciplines for the application of anti-dumping measures, injury determinations have been defined more precisely and a new "sunset review" clause limits the duration of duties, subject to review. The importance of having a clear and adequate multilateral framework of rules in this area can be seen *e.g.* from the fact that both OECD and non-OECD countries are using and are affected by anti-dumping actions fairly widely (see Table 4.5). The new Uruguay Round Agreement on Subsides and Countervailing Measures prescribes more clearly the circumstances and rules governing countervailing duty actions and strengthens notification and surveillance procedures with respect to subsidies. More precise global rules in these areas lead to more consistent practices and procedures throughout the world.

- The WTO Agreement on Implementation of Article VII of the GATT 1994 (known also as the Agreement on Customs Valuation) sets forth rules intended to provide a fair, uniform and neutral system for customs valuation for all WTO members that precludes the use of arbitrary or fictitious customs values. The need for disciplines in this area arises as certain practices, such as arbitrary intervention on the part of customs authorities or mis-declarations by importers about actual prices of goods in order to reduce customs duty payments, can result in uncertainty about expected customs duty on an imported product and stifle trade. The Agreement is therefore in the interest of all WTO members and their importers.

At the same time, there have been concerns expressed particularly by various non-OECD countries. Some cite excessively burdensome implementation problems in some areas, compounded by a perception that many of the provisions provided in various Agreements to safeguard the interests of "developing countries" have not adequately addressed their concerns.

Some non-OECD countries feel that the implementation of the TRIMs Agreement has posed several problems for them. These countries have expressed concerns about the adequacy of the transitional period for phasing out TRIMs, and have called for extension of compliance deadlines. Especially, they point to the importance of local content requirements in their development policies, in particular in relation to the automotive sector.

Moreover, several non-OECD countries have argued that IP protection under the TRIPs Agreement is largely oriented towards areas of interest to developed countries, leaving aside areas that particularly interest other countries, like indigenous knowledge or geographical indications for traditional handicrafts. Moreover, some countries point out that compliance with the Agreement is particularly difficult for "developing countries," given that most of them had to start work on IPRs from scratch and lack the necessary human resources and expertise.

Concerning anti-dumping, some non-OECD countries have expressed concerns about the number of anti-dumping measures against their products and their harassing effects. However, it is interesting to note that between 1995 and 1999, non-OECD countries have filed a total of 632 anti-dumping cases against 595 filed by OECD countries (Table 4.5). Of those filed by non-OECD countries, a total of 301 anti-dumping cases were filed against OECD countries, and 331 against each other. On the other hand, of the 595 anti-dumping cases that were filed by OECD countries, 335 were directed against non-OECD countries and 260 against other OECD countries. Moreover, non-OECD countries have expressed fear that anti-dumping measures may critically increase in the textiles and clothing sector. These countries have called for a prohibition of repeated anti-dumping investigations on the same product within a year, as well as for making it mandatory rather than "desirable" to impose a smaller margin of anti-dumping duty when this would suffice to remove injury from domestic industry. It is worth mentioning that anti-dumping procedures are resource-intensive, and as such, they tend to weigh more heavily on small-sized economies than on others. Moreover, for countries whose exports are concentrated in relatively few sectors, anti-dumping duties may have a disproportionate impact on their economies. Finally, a number of non-OECD countries are negotiating extensions of time to implement the Customs Valuation Agreement, citing resource limitations within the customs services and concerns over potential revenue losses.

Not only does the WTO encompass new rules and strengthened disciplines in such areas through the Uruguay Round, but it also provides systems for surveying the operation of those disciplines and for discussing problems or issues that may arise, including the Council for Trade in Goods, the Council for TRIPs and the Anti-dumping Committee that are tackling the concerns mentioned above. Simultaneously, the strengthening of dispute settlement procedures in the WTO has greatly enhanced the credibility and integrity of multilateral trade disciplines and provided a more reliable mechanism for dealing with trade conflicts and disputes.

D. The impact of the Uruguay Round and beyond

(i) Overall welfare gains

In order to help put things in perspective, it is instructive to review some of the studies that have attempted to estimate empirically the economic impact of the Uruguay Round and of various post-Uruguay liberalisation scenarios. The results of the models discussed here are estimations of the potential net welfare gains from trade liberalisation. These are calculated from estimated net efficiency gains and net terms of trade effects, net of the effects of induced changes in tariff revenues. They therefore should be read as "bottom line" results. The calculations attempt to capture both the aggregate gains and losses from structural adjustments that would follow from liberalisation. They are not forecasts of what to expect by way of changes in welfare, but rather estimates of the net results of trade liberalisation compared with what would have been obtained in its absence.

The Uruguay Round creates major difficulties for economic modelling. This is because it goes well beyond cutting protection on trade in goods to include services, investment, and intellectual property, and because many of its effects will operate through an improved system of multilateral rules and disciplines.[13] All modelling exercises use simplifying assumptions to make quantification more tractable. Some assumptions result in under-estimation of the positive effects of trade liberalisation. In particular, many areas cannot be captured through modelling exercises. These include scale economies, specialisation, and the positive effect on confidence that the conclusion of the Uruguay Round has brought. The calculations of the Uruguay Round implementation also omit the benefits from liberalisation in services and investment, protection of intellectual property, and strengthening of rules governing trade remedies such as anti-dumping and countervailing duties. As will be described below, the addition of services alone under the GATT/WTO umbrella is expected to lead to substantial benefits, as the service sector is now the largest sector in most economies, OECD and non-OECD. The calculations also do not capture the positive contribution to trade liberalisation made by the increasing application of multilateral disciplines by the non-OECD countries or by their unilateral liberalisation in the context of accession to the GATT/WTO.

With these caveats in mind, Table 4.4 presents a summary of the main results of recent studies as well as the model type and liberalisation assumptions used in each of these.

The impact on world welfare of the Uruguay Round implementation is estimated to range between $40 billion (Francois et al., 1995) and $93 billion (Harrison et al., 1995) when using comparative static models with perfect competition and constant returns to scale. Using the same assumptions, Nguyen *et al.* (1993) obtain larger welfare gains ($212 billion) as they consider a more generous liberalisation package than the one actually achieved by the Uruguay Round.

Static models which assume imperfect competition and increasing returns to scale report higher results from the Uruguay Round implementation since, unlike the approaches in the above-cited papers, they also consider additional channels for gains from trade trough increased competition, scale economies and product variety. Welfare gains have been estimated to reach values between $93 billion (Francois *et al.*, 1995) or $96 billion (Harrison *et al.*, 1995) and $158 billion (Chadha *et al.* (2000). The results they all obtain translate to comparable impacts on welfare: the first two studies estimate a 0.4% increase in global GDP, while the latter one finds a 0.5% increase in real GDP. The gains to non-OECD countries range from $19 billion, or 0.5% increase in their GDP (Harrison *et al.*, 1997) to $108 billion, or 0.8% increase in their GDP (Chadha *et al.,*2000).

When taking into account dynamic effects, the estimated gains from the Uruguay Round reach higher values ranging between $258 billion (Hertel *et al.*, 1995) and $510 billion (Francois *et al.*, 1994). These figures translate into a net increase in world income from 0.9% to 2% of world real GDP.

Studies which simulate various post-Uruguay liberalisation scenarios report static welfare gains ranging between $82 billion or 0.2% increase in GDP (OECD 1999) to $836 billion or 2.5% increase in GDP (Chadha *et al.*, 2000). Dynamic post-Uruguay welfare gains reach higher values between $688 billion or 2.1% increase in GDP (Chadha *et al.*, 2000) and $1212 billion or 3.1% from GDP (OECD 1999).

While different models using different modelling assumptions and liberalisation scenarios can lead to differences in results, they nonetheless illustrate that global welfare impacts of trade liberalisation are significant. While the largest welfare gains in *absolute* terms accrue to OECD countries, non-OECD countries gain more relative to their GDPs.[14] It is also the case that benefits from trade liberalisation are commensurate with countries' own efforts: the deeper the cuts in protection, the larger are the net benefits.

(ii) Services liberalisation

The majority of existing general equilibrium assessments of services trade liberalisation do not explicitly model the different modes of services supply, employing models used to simulate goods liberalisation, but implicitly include the reduction of barriers in all modes of supply in considering services liberalisation.[15] The studies use estimates of tariff equivalents for services barriers constructed by Hoekman (1996) on the basis of scheduled commitments under GATS using the frequency index methodology.

There are only two studies (Dee and Hanslow, 2000, and Verikios and Zhang, 2000) that incorporate explicitly trade in services through commercial presence (FDI), substantially improving the framework for modelling services. They also use improved estimates for services barriers, which draw on more comprehensive databases of measures affecting trade in services and reflect the economic impact of services barriers on prices or quantities.[16]

A rigorous comparison in the range and quality of the different results is difficult given that the models employed for quantifying the welfare effects from services liberalisation make different assumptions with respect to the underlying modelling structure, the distortion data for services sectors and the liberalisation scenarios considered (ranging from a 33% cut in services protection to a total elimination of services barriers). In addition, the difficulties arising from poor information on international services transactions and on prevailing services barriers and their economic effect suggest that results should be interpreted with care.

However, all studies show that liberalisation of trade in services generates substantial welfare gains. These are at least of the same order of magnitude as those derived from goods liberalisation, in some cases exceeding them significantly.[17] [18]

As for the regional distribution of the welfare effects, empirical studies show that, generally economies with initial high protection levels tend to gain most (in terms of percentage gains to GDP). As the values of estimates for services trade barriers are relatively higher for non-OECD countries than for OECD countries, this suggests that the former are potentially the major winners from services liberalisation.

Table 4.1. **Pre and post Uruguay Round trade-weighted average tariff rates, by country of origin and destination**

	Destination					
Origin	OECD countries			Non-OECD countries		
	Pre-UR	Post-UR	Reduction	Pre-UR	Post-UR	Reduction
OECD	5.5	3.0	45	14.9	10.7	28
US	4.4	1.9	57	13.6	10.2	25
EU	5.8	3.5	40	18.4	13.8	25
Japan	6.2	3.6	42	14.1	9.3	34
Other	4.9	2.4	51	12.4	9.0	35
Non-OECD	6.9	4.8	30	10.0	7.1	29
Latin America	4.4	3.2	27	13.4	10.1	25
Asia	7.8	5.2	33	9.6	6.7	30
Africa	8.4	6.7	20	2.5	1.1	56
Europe	9.5	7.3	23	18.6	14.9	20

Source: OECD, *Tariffs and Trade database*

Table 4.2. OECD country tariff profiles by industrial product groups

Product category	Percentage of imports											
	Duty-free		0.1-5%		5.1-10%		10.1-15%		15.1-35%		Over 35%	
	Pre-	Post-	Pre-	Post-	Pre-	Post-	Pre-	Post-	Pre-	Post-	Pre-	Post-
All industrial products (excluding petroleum)	20	43	41	33	24	15	7	5	6	4	1	1
Textiles and clothing	2	4	6	14	27	29	30	25	33	27	2	1
Metals	36	70	36	21	23	7	3	1	2	1	1	0
Mineral products & precious stones	59	81	28	9	10	9	3	1	2	1	0	0
Electric machinery	5	30	54	55	26	6	11	7	3	2	1	0
Leather, rubber, footwear & travel goods	16	19	17	29	47	37	7	4	11	9	3	2
Wood, pulp, paper & furniture	50	84	24	6	20	7	2	2	4	0	1	0
Fish & fish products	21	24	42	44	18	21	18	8	7	3	0	0
Non-electric machinery	11	48	74	42	10	7	2	1	2	2	1	0
Chemicals & photographic supplies	14	34	31	27	40	37	10	2	5	1	1	0
Transport equipment	16	21	52	50	21	19	2	2	5	4	4	3
Manufactured articles n.e.s.	15	49	38	37	40	10	5	3	2	1	0	0

Source: OECD, *Tariffs and Trade database*

Table 4.3. **The effects of Uruguay Round concessions on tariff escalation in OECD countries**

		Tariff rate			Change in escalation indicator[1]	
Processing stage	Description	Pre-Uruguay	Post-Uruguay	Absolute reduction	Stage comparison	Absolute difference
	Hides, skins and leather	5.2	4.2	1.0		
1	Raw hides	0.1	0.1	0.0		
2	Semi-manufactures	4.5	3.5	1.1	2 with 1	Decreased
3	Finished products	8.7	7.3	1.5	3 with 2	Increased
	Rubber	3.3	2.2	1.1		
1	Crude rubber	0.0	0.0	0.0		
2	Semi-manufactures	5.5	3.2	2.3	2 with 1	Decreased
3	Finished products	5.1	3.5	1.6	3 with 2	Decreased
	Wood	2.0	0.9	1.1		
1	Wood in the rough	0.0	0.0	0.0		
2	Wood Based Panels	9.4	5.4	4.0	2 with 1	Decreased
3	Semi-manufactures	0.9	0.4	0.4	3 with 2	--
4	Wood articles	4.7	0.5	4.3	4 with 3	Decreased
	Paper	3.5	1.5	2.0		
1	Pulp and Waste	0.0	0.0	0.0		
2	Paper and paperboard	5.3	2.6	2.7	2 with 1	Decreased
3	Printed matter	1.7	0.3	1.4	3 with 2	--
4	Paper articles	7.3	1.9	5.4	4 with 3	Decreased
	Jute	5.1	1.8	3.2		
1	Jute fibers	0.0	0.0	0.0		
2	Yarns of jute	5.4	0.1	5.2	2 with 1	Decreased
3	Jute fabrics	5.7	3.2	2.5	3 with 2	Increased
	Cocoa	4.4	2.5	1.9		
1	Cocoa beans	2.1	0.0	2.1		
2	Paste, powder and butter	4.6	2.8	1.8	2 with 1	Increased
3	Chocolate	8.8	7.2	1.6	3 with 2	Increased

Source: OECD, *Tariffs and Trade database*

Table 4.4. **Global general equilibrium studies of multilateral trade liberalisation**

Study/model	Base year/projection year	Model structure	Liberalisation assumptions (UR implementation/ post UR liberalisation)	Welfare effects
Anderson *et al.* (2000)	Projections of the database from 1995 to 2005.	GTAP model of global trade, with perfect competition and constant returns to scale	Only Post-Uruguay liberalisation scenarios: • Completion of manufacturing tariff cuts under the UR, • Implementation of the Agreement on Textiles and Clothing and • Accession of' China & Chinese Taipei to the WTO	Total welfare gains: $254.3 billion (1995 dollars measured in 2005) • Developing countries: $108.1 (or 42.5% from total gains) • Developed countries: $146.2 billion (or 57.5 % from total gains)
Chadha, Brown, Deardorff and Stern (2000)	For UR implementation: GTAP data 1995	Michigan Model of World Production and Trade with imperfect competition, increasing returns to scale and product heterogeneity	Implementation of the Uruguay Round: • Reduction of import tariffs on agriculture, mining and manufacturing sectors • Complete elimination of export-tax equivalents by all countries in these sectors • Removal of MFA quota restraints,	Total gains from UR implementation $159.7 billion (1995 dollars) or 0.5% increase in welfare • Developing countries: $44.1 billion or 0.8% increase in welfare • Developed countries: $115.5 billion or 0.4% increase in welfare

	For Post-UR liberalisation: updated post-UR database to the year 2005		Post-Uruguay liberalisation scenarios:
			• Separate and simultaneous 33% reduction in remaining barriers in all sectors:
			  • agriculture,
			  • mining and manufactures, and
			  • services
				Total gains from Post-Uruguay liberalisation scenarios: $835.8 billion or 2.5% increase in welfare
				• Developing countries: $179.8 billion (3.2%)
				• Developed countries: $656 billion (2.4%)
				Gains from *services* sectors liberalisation: $687.9 billion or 2.1% increase in welfare
				• Developing countries $137 billion (2.5%)
				• Developed countries $550.7 billion (2.0%)

(continued)

Table 4.4. **Global general equilibrium studies of multilateral trade liberalisation** (continued)

Study/model	Base year/projection year	Model structure	Liberalisation assumptions (UR implementation/ post UR liberalisation)	Welfare effects
Dee and Hanslow (2000)	Updated GTAP version 4 (1995) following a simulation which implements the UR results under a scenario provided by Verikios and Hanslow (1999) FDI data 1994/1995	FTAP model: version of the GTAP model with capital mobility and FDI, increasing returns to scale and large-group monopolistic competition in all sectors	Only Post-UR liberalisation • elimination of post-UR tariffs for agricultural and manufactured products and • elimination of post-UR estimates in services sectors	Global welfare effects: $266.9 billion (1995 dollars) • $133.5 billion from agricultural and manufactured products liberalisation • $133.4 billion from services liberalisation (or 0.46% of world real income)
Verikios and Zhang (2000)	Updated GTAP version 4 (1995) following a simulation which implements the UR results under a scenario provided by Verikios and Hanslow (1999) FDI data 1994/1995	FTAP model: version of the GTAP model with capital mobility and FDI, increasing returns to scale and large-group monopolistic competition in all sectors (greater sectoral detail for services sectors)	Only Post-UR services liberalisation scenarios: Elimination of barriers to trade in • communication services • financial services in a post-Uruguay environment	• $12.7 billion (or 0.05 increase in real income) • $3.5 billion (or 0.01 increase in real income)

(continued)

Table 4.4. **Global general equilibrium studies of multilateral trade liberalisation** (continued)

Study/model	Base year/projection year	Model structure	Liberalisation assumptions (UR implementation/ post UR liberalisation)	Welfare effects
Australian Department of Foreign Affaires and Trade (1999)	GTAP version 4, reference year 1995	GTAP comparative static CGE, perfect competition and constant returns to scale APG Cubed dynamic model	Post-UR liberalisation scenarios • Cut of 50% in agriculture, manufactures and services distortions • Elimination of barriers in all sectors • APG-Cubed mode: removal of protection over the five years from 2004	• Global gains: over $406 billion -- $250 billion (62%) from services; $66 billion (16%) from manufactures; $90 billion (22%) from agriculture • Over $750 billion • APG-Cubed model: additional welfare gains of $600 billion in 2008 when removing protection over 5 years from 2004
OECD Development Centre (1999)	GTAP database version 4 (1995) and growth projections provided by the World Bank; protection level: 1995, which reflects partial UR implementation	Trade Policy Simulation Model: a dynamic general equilibrium model with constant returns to scale and perfect competition	Only post-UR liberalisation (3 scenarios). Results are reported only for the full liberalisation scenario: • complete elimination of tariffs for agricultural and industrial products for both OECD and non-OECD economies	Static welfare gains: $82 billion (in 1995 prices) or 0.2% of GDP: • OECD countries $64 billion (0.2% of GDP) • non-OECD: $18 billion (0.2% of GDP) Dynamic welfare gains (with endogenous total factor productivity): $1 212 billion or 3.1% of GDP: • OECD countries $757 billion (or 2.5% of GDP) and • non-OECD: $455 billion (or 4.9% of GDP)
Hertel and Martin (1999)	GTAP database version 4, base year 1995	Standard multi region applied general equilibrium model with perfect competition & constant returns to scale & imperfect competition & economies of scale	Only post-UR liberalisation scenarios: Separate and simultaneous 33% reduction of the post-Uruguay protection level for • manufactures • agricultural products • services	Welfare gains from liberalising • Manufactures: $22 billion (almost doubles when considering imperfect competition) • agriculture: $27 billion, • services $140 billion

(continued)

Table 4.4. **Global general equilibrium studies of multilateral trade liberalisation** (continued)

Study/model	Base year/projection year	Model structure	Liberalisation assumptions (UR implementation/ post UR liberalisation)	Welfare effects
Robinson et al.(1999)	GTAP version 4, reference year 1995	comparative static CGE, perfect competition and constant returns to scale	Post-UR multilateral liberalisation: • 50% cut in food, agriculture and natural resources and 100% cut in manufactures • additional 50% cut in services sectors distortions	Total welfare gains: 1.62% change from base year GDP • 0.20% change from base year GDP • 1.05% change from base year GDP
Francois and McDonald (1997)	GTAP version 3, 1992	The model covers all world trade and production; it allows for scale economies and imperfect competition; and it allows for trade to affect capital stocks through investment effects.	Uruguay Round implementation: • industrial NTB elimination modelled trough export taxes (including the MFA and EU restrictions on Japanese automobile exports); • industrial tariff reductions as scheduled; • liberalisation of agriculture trade; and • new government procurement provisions Post Uruguay liberalisation : • free trade in information technologies • hypothetical further reduction in agricultural border interventions from UR levels and in the level of all industrial tariffs; and • an expansion of the AGP to all WTO members, involving a 50% reduction in estimated preference margins for core government demand	Real income effects from UR implementation: $315.6 billion of 1992 dollars Total welfare gains from post-UR liberalisation: $446.1 billions of 1992 dollars ($206.1 billion when reductions are undertaken only by OECD members).

(continued)

Table 4.4. **Global general equilibrium studies of multilateral trade liberalisation** (continued)

Study/model	Base year/projection year	Model structure	Liberalisation assumptions (UR implementation/ post UR liberalisation)	Welfare effects
Harrison, Rutherford, Tarr (1997)	GTAP database for 1992 (version 2)	Static and dynamic model with • Constant returns to scale (CRTS) and perfect competition • Increasing returns to scale (IRTS) and imperfect competition	Only UR implementation: Protection reduction in manufactures and agriculture according to the actual agreed offers: • tariff reductions in manufactured products • reduction of protection level in agriculture • reduction of export and production subsides in agriculture • elimination of Voluntary Export Restraints and the MFA	Static welfare effects (in 1992 dollars) $93 billion annually (CRTS) • Developing countries $17.7 billion (or 0.4% from GDP) and • Developed countries $75.2 for (or 0.4% from GDP) $96 billion annually (IRTS) • Developing countries $19.4 billion (or 0.5% from GDP) and • Developed countries $76.7 for (or 0.5% from GDP) Dynamic welfare effects: $171 billion annually • Developing countries $55.2 billion (or 1.4% from GDP) • Developed countries and $115.4 (or 0.8% from GDP)
Brown, Deardorff, Fox and Stern (1995)	1990	Michigan model of world production & trade, perfectly competitive agricultural sector; monopolistically competitive manufacturing and services sectors	UR implementation: Cut in tariff rates on industrial and agricultural products in concordance with the agreed offers; Post-UR liberalisation : For services: an additional 25% reduction in post-Uruguay Round services sector ad valorem tariff equivalents rates	Welfare effect as a percentage change: UR/post-UR US : 0.3 (UR) / 0.9 (post-UR) Canada: 0.4 / 2.0 Mexico: 0.1 / 2.8 Europe: 0.3 / 0.9 Japan: 0.6 / 1.4 Asian newly industrialised: 2.4 / 3.6 Australia, New Zealand: 1.2 / 3.9 Other trading nations: 0.0 / 1.0
Hertel, Martin, Yanagashima & Dimaranan (1995)	GTAP version 2, 1992/projection of the world economy 2005	Constant returns to scale, perfect competition	Only UR implementation: Industrial tariff cuts according to schedules, protection in agriculture reduced according to the Agreement on Agriculture, elimination of MFA quotas	Total gains: 0.89% of projected 2005 expenditure level $258 billion in 1992 dollars, measured in 2005

(continued)

Table 4.4. **Global general equilibrium studies of multilateral trade liberalisation** (continued)

Study/model	Base year/projection year	Model structure	Liberalisation assumptions (UR implementation/ post UR liberalisation)	Welfare effects
Francois, McDonald and Nordstrom (1994/1995)	GTAP version 2, 1992	• Constant returns to scale (CRTS), perfect competition • Scale economies (IRTS), imperfect competition.	Only UR implementation: Calculations based on the final offer data.	Welfare effects based on 1994 study $510 billion (1992 dollars, measured in 2005) Welfare effects based on 1994 study (billion, 1992 dollars and percentage of GDP) CRTS / IRTS Fixed capital stock: $ 39.65 (0.17%) / $ 99.4 (0.44%) Endogenous capital stock fixed savings rate: $ 64.85 (0.29%) / $192.6 (0.85%) Endogenous capital stock, endogenous savings rate: $102.9 (0.45%) / $214.4 (0.94%)
Haaland and Tollefsen (1994)	1985/1992	Combination of perfectly competitive market sand imperfectly competitive markets	UR implementation based on projections of stylised scenarios, not on actual agreed offers. Static liberalisation cases: • A 33% cut in tariffs and NTBs for manufactures • A 33% cut in services barriers (assumed to have a value of 15%). Dynamic liberalisation: same scenarios but considers also additional dynamic effects from endogenous investments	Static welfare effects (change from base case in million 1985 ECU) • Manufactures liberalisation: mil. ECU 12.606 • Services liberalisation: mil. ECU 4.714 • Total liberalisation: mil. ECU 17.334 (or 0.17 % increase in world income - GDP weighted) Dynamic welfare effects from total liberalisation: mil. ECU 22.474 (or 0.21 % increase in world income - GDP weighted)
OECD (1993)		Constant returns to scale in production; perfect competition.	Calculations based on the DFA, manufacturing tariffs and NTBs cut by 36%; agricultural subsidies by 36% & agricultural support cut by 20%	$274 billion (1992 dollars, measured in 2002) • Developed countries: $188 billion • Developing countries $86 billion

(continued)

Table 4.4. **Global general equilibrium studies of multilateral trade liberalisation** (continued)

Study/model	Base year/projection year	Model structure	Liberalisation assumptions (UR implementation/ post UR liberalisation)	Welfare effects
Nguyen, Perroni and Wigle (1993)		Constant returns to scale in production; perfect competition.	Partial MFA liberalisation; cut in both agricultural subsidies & support by 70%; reduction of import tariffs on industrial goods by 50%.	$212 billion
DRI (1993)		Macro-econometric, partial equilibrium model of the G7 with efficiency gains from trade liberalisation exogenously determined.		increase of 4.5% in world income
Stoeckel (1990)		Constant returns to scale in production; perfect competition.	Tariff & NTBs reduced by half.	increase of 5.0% in world income
Peterson (1992)		Global macro-econometric, partial equilibrium model with product differentiation & constant returns to scale in production.		increase of 1.0% in world income

Table 4.5. **Anti-dumping actions**

A. Initiations of anti-dumping investigations: reporting and affected countries by level of development, 1995-1999

Affected country	OECD	Non-OECD	Total
Reporting country			
OECD	260	335	595
Percentage	*44*	*56*	*100*
Non-OECD	301	331	632
Percentage	*48*	*52*	*100*
Total number of initiations			1227

B. Definitive anti-dumping measures: reporting and affected countries by level of development, 1995-1999

Affected country	OECD	Non-OECD	Total
Reporting country			
OECD	133	208	341
Percentage	*39*	*61*	*100*
Non-OECD	107	179	286
Percentage	*37*	*63*	*100*
Total number of measures			627

Notes:

Non-OECD countries subject to or initiating antidumping actions recorded in the WTO database between 1995 and 1999 are the following: Algeria, Argentina, Bahrain, Belarus, Bosnia Herzegovina, Brazil, Bulgaria, Chile, China, Chinese Taipei, Colombia, Costa Rica, Croatia, Cuba, Ecuador, Egypt, Estonia, Guatemala, Honduras, Hong Kong-China, India, Indonesia, Israel, Kazakstan, Latvia, Lithuania, Liechtenstein, Macao, Macedonia, Malawi, Malaysia, Moldova, Mozambique, Nicaragua, Pakistan, Panama, Paraguay, Peru, Philippines, Romania, Russia, Saudi Arabia, Singapore, Slovenia, South Africa, Thailand, Trinidad and Tobago, Ukraine, United Arab Emirates, Uruguay, Uzbekistan, Venezuela, Vietnam, Yugoslavia and Zimbabwe

Source: WTO Secretariat, Rules Division Antidumping Measures Database. Data for 1999 included here are preliminary.

Notes

1 This is in fact the classic dilemma for trade policy reforms where governments appear to behave as if imports are intrinsically undersirable and economically costly, while exports are virtuous.

2 Executives were asked about the degree to which economies did *not* appear to have hidden trade barriers. Those responses appear to be positively correlated with GDP per capita. Hence, the interpretation that lower degrees of hidden barriers are positively correlated with GDP per capita. See additional information in the notes to the figure. Note that the groups of economies identified in the figure as "Quad", "Other OECD" and "selected non-OECD" correspond to the same country groupings used in Tables 13 and 14 below.

3 Low and Yeats, "Non-tariff measures and developing countries: Has the Uruguay Round Levelled the Playing Fields?", World Bank Policy Research Working Paper No. 1353, 1994.

4 GATT, An analysis of the proposed Uruguay Round agreements, with particular emphasis on aspects of interest to developing countries, Document MTN.TNC/W/122, MTN.GNG/W/30 (29 November 1993).

5 Allan V. Deardorff, "Economic effects of tariff and quota reductions", in: The New GATT: Implications for the United States, edited by Susan M. Collins and Barry P. Bosworth, Brookings 1994, p. 19.

6 The World Bank: 'The World Development Report', 1999/2000.

7 Recent OECD work has identified barriers to trade in services in the following sectors: wholesale trade services (TD/TC/WP(99)18/FINAL); retail trade services (TD/TC/WP(99)41/FINAL); financial information services (TD/TC/WP(98)51/FINAL and ANNEX); tourism (TD/TC/WP(2000)10/FINAL); environmental services (COM/TD/ENV(2000)86/FINAL) and air cargo (TD/TC/WP(99)57/FINAL).

8 Setting targets for expanded coverage to be achieved in the next round would help provide a focal point for policy makers. Quantitative indicators that could be considered include the share of sectors that have been scheduled, and the share of commitments that involve a bound promise not to apply any national treatment or market access violating measures. Both indicators do not require any judgement regarding the importance of actual policies that restrict national treatment or market access, whether or not scheduled (see "Cross-cutting ("Formula") Approaches to Multilateral Services Negotiations," - TD/TC/WP(99)42/FINAL). One problem with formula-based approaches to expanding coverage is that sectors that are important inputs into production and sectors where barriers to trade and investment are currently highest may remain excluded, in both developed and developing countries. Consequently, request-offer negotiations of the type used in the first round of GATS talks cannot and should not be avoided.

9 During recent GATS-based negotiations on basic telecommunications and financial services, several governments took advantage of the GATS to balance their reluctance to unleash competition immediately on protected national suppliers, and their desire not to be held hostage in perpetuity either to the weakness of domestic industry or to pressure from vested interests. This was most striking in the case of basic telecommunications, where a number of African, Latin American and Caribbean countries bound themselves to introduce competition at precise future dates. For several countries, this signalled the end of the exclusive rights granted for many years to a foreign monopolist or dominant

supplier. The use of the GATS as a mechanism for lending credibility to financial sector liberalisation programmes has been less prevalent, in part because financial services markets tend to be more competitive than basic telecommunications and because the negotiations were concluded at a time of considerable uncertainty in financial markets (Mattoo, 1999b).

10 See "Using "Cluster" Approaches to Specific Commitments for Interdependent Services" (TD/TC/WP(2000)9/FINAL).

11 This is particularly so as one of the key instruments used to restrict trade through this mode of supply involves quantity-based policy tools (through visa quotas). These can be expanded over time, with "within quota" visas not being subject to economic needs tests, and possibly with liberalisation facilitated by a mode 4-specific safeguard procedure. For detailed proposals by developing country scholars in this area, see Chanda (1999) and Mukherjee (1999).

12 Article 2.1 of the TRIMs Agreement requires Members not to apply any TRIM that is inconsistent with the provisions of Article III (national treatment of imported products) or Article XI (prohibition of quantitative restrictions on imports or exports) of GATT 1994.

13 For a comprehensive analysis of the benefits to non-OECD countries from the Uruguay Round, see Safadi, Raed and Sam Laird, "The Uruguay Round and Developing Countries," *Journal of World Development*, Vol. 24, No. 7, July 1996.

14 See in particular, Dessus, S., Fukasaku, K. and Safadi, R., Multilateral Trade Liberalisation and the Developing Countries , 1999. OECD Development Centre Policy Brief No. 18, Paris, October.

15 Chadha, Brown, Deardorff and Stern (2000), Australian Department of Foreign Affairs and Trade (1999), Robinson et al.(1999), Brown, Deardorff, Fox and Stern (1995). For a survey of the literature that has attempted to quantify the welfare benefits from services trade liberalisation, see OECD (2000), Quantification of Costs to National Welfare from Barriers to Services Trade TD/TC/WP(2000)24/REV1.

16 Estimates for services barriers are taken from Kalirajan *et al.* (2000), who estimated the impact of barriers to trade in banking services on prices, and from Warren (2000), who estimated the impact of barriers to trade in telecommunication services on quantities of telecommunication services delivered which he subsequently transformed into price impacts.

17 Dee and Hanslow (2000)

18 For example, Robinson *et al.* (1999) found that the welfare gain for the world as a whole from a 50 percent cut in services sectors is five times larger than that from non-services sectors trade liberalisation.

V. THE WTO AND DEVELOPMENT

Four important propositions have thus far been established:

(i) Trade is important to non-OECD countries since it is often the primary mean for achieving global integration.
(ii) Trade liberalisation contributes to economic development, but is no substitute for good development policies.
(iii) The trading interests of non-OECD countries are better served in the context of the multilateral trading system that promotes and maintains liberal trade regimes buttressed by transparent, predictable and enforceable international trade rules.
(iv) The global trends, while positive overall, have not benefited non-OECD countries equally.

While improvements in market access conditions, as described in the previous Chapter, hold the promise for further benefits to accrue from multilateral liberalisation efforts, it is worth noting that the majority of non-OECD countries benefit from preferential access to many OECD markets, and an even more favourable access is granted to the poorer countries. What follows is an attempt to describe the actual and potential role the WTO could play to help countries with their integration efforts.

More than two-thirds of the WTO current 140-strong members are developing countries.[1] Despite extensive references in the WTO Agreements to special provisions, rights and obligations accorded to developing countries, there is no official definition of what constitutes a "developing country." Rather, GATT Contracting Parties have self-elected their designation, most recently when the WTO was created.[2] However, there is an official list of UN-designated least-developed countries (LDCs) that includes a total of 48 countries, of which 29 are WTO members (Appendix 2 examines in detail LDCs' trade performance). In the remainder of the study, reference to developing countries follows WTO practice.

Prior to the Uruguay Round, developing countries received special and differential treatment (S&D) in six different areas. One from Article XVIII of GATT 1947 that gave developing countries the right to protect infant industries and to use trade restrictions for balance-of-payments purposes. Another from three articles (XXXVI, XXXVII and XXXVIII) under Part IV of GATT 1964 that recognised the special needs of developing countries in the trading system and exempted them from making reciprocal tariff concessions. And four in the context of the 1979 framework agreement, commonly known as the Enabling Clause.

Under the Enabling Clause, specific legal cover was provided for the Generalised System of Preferences (GSP), for special and differential treatment under the Tokyo Round Codes, for regional arrangements among developing countries, and for special treatment in favour of the least developed countries. Two other features of the Enabling Clause deserve mention here. These are the juxtaposed statements on reciprocity and graduation. On the one hand, the Enabling Clause states that industrial countries do not expect to receive reciprocal commitments from developing countries that are inconsistent with the latter's individual development, financial and trade needs. On the other hand, the

Enabling Clause also states that developing countries expect to participate more fully in the framework of GATT rights and obligations as their development and trade situation improves.

In short, S&D up until the Uruguay Round rested on two pillars. One conferred on developing countries special treatment under the rules, and preferential access to OECD markets. Non-reciprocity in trade negotiations and graduation formed the other pillar.

The Uruguay Round chipped away at the two pillars of S&D, though neither was completely stripped. Preferential access continues to apply independently of the outcome of the Uruguay Round, while special treatment under the rules has been constrained.

As described earlier, the Uruguay Round results embodied in the Marrakech Agreement Establishing the World Trade Organisation and the Annexes to that Agreement and the associated Ministerial Decisions, Declarations and Understandings are a "single undertaking" to which all WTO members subscribe. Thus, in practice non-reciprocity in trade negotiations under Part IV no longer applies as every WTO member has to submit schedules of bindings in goods and in services.

In recognition of special difficulties in implementation of some of the agreements and associated adjustment costs, additional S&D provisions were introduced, bringing the total to 145.[3] Within these provisions, more benefits were targeted towards least developed countries, net food importing developing countries (NFIDCs), and Annex VII Countries (defined as those with a per capita income less than $1000).

A. Developing countries' concerns

Most of the new S&D provisions were introduced to help developing countries implement the new agreements and to alleviate the burden of adjustment. As such, S&D provisions have in effect triggered a debate on the special problems and barriers that developing countries face as they seek fuller integration into the world economy. And by including additional benefits in favour of least developed, Annex VII countries and net food importing developing countries, the Uruguay Round has also opened the door on the concept of tiering of S&D benefits across different groups of developing countries.

Following WTO practice, concerns over the different provisions included in S&D have been grouped under five main headings: (1) provisions aimed at increasing developing countries' trade opportunities; (2) provisions that call upon WTO members to safeguard the interest of developing countries; (3) flexibility of commitments; (4) transitional time periods; and (5) technical assistance. As will be described below, developing countries have raised concerns under each of the headings, except in the case of flexibility in commitments.

(i) Provisions to increase trade opportunities

a. Preferential access

The Generalised System of Preferences (GSP) is the most extensive and explicit expression of an attempt to use trade preferences as a tool of development. It is a scheme under which all developing countries are supposedly eligible for trade preferences where preference-giving countries exempt imports from developing countries from MFN duties. The GSP was founded on three principles - that it be "generalised," non-discriminatory and non-reciprocal. However, the unilateral, non-contractual basis on which preference-giving countries have always maintained their GSP schemes has meant that in practice, not all of these principles have been fully observed in all of the schemes.

Considering that GSP has always been regarded as a temporary phenomenon, or as a mechanism to help developing countries "catch up" with their industrial country counterparts, it is hardly surprising that the notion that GSP should be generalised and non-discriminatory has given rise to interpretative differences. If GSP is to be transient, countries and/or products must inevitably be graduated from preferences over time. And since GSP is unilateral, consistency as to the coverage of schemes can hardly be expected. Product and country exceptions, variations in eligibility rules, different approaches to the determination of preference margins, and an assortment of conditionalities all add to the heterogeneity of the schemes.

In theory, preferences can increase the exports of a recipient country, but if the expansion derives from trade diversion rather than trade creation, it will be at the cost of the preference-giving country and third parties. Export expansion in beneficiary countries may contribute to development in a broad sense, via increased investment, growth and employment, and diversification of the production base away from exclusive reliance on production of primary goods. The non-preferential creation of new market access opportunities would hold out the same promise, but with the vital difference that no particular country or group of countries would be accorded such opportunities to the exclusion of others. This competitive "edge" provided by preferences, supposedly on a temporary basis, is generally justified as a mechanism to help developing countries catch up with their more developed counterparts.

Two obvious disadvantages in using preferences as a means of according a temporary economic advantage are, firstly, that the preferences may induce beneficiaries to specialise in activities in which they will never be competitive, and secondly, that they create vested interests opposed to multilateral trade liberalisation. Inappropriate specialisation may be particularly acute where preferential access entails economic transfers arising from privileged access behind high non-tariff barriers, as has been the case, for example, with certain agricultural preferences. Not only is the reversal of reliance on such high rent transfers likely to prove extremely painful unless it is carefully managed over an extended period, but the preferences themselves have perpetuated mono-cultural dependence rather than promoting diversification of the production base. This observation leads to the conclusion that preference margins can be too high for the long-term good of beneficiaries.

Most available research suggest that with the exception of a few of the larger developing countries, and in relation to a few products, the preference schemes have had limited success in generating significant export growth or improving the trade shares of beneficiaries. By extension, the effects of preferences on income levels and economic growth have not been great for the majority of beneficiaries. While it appears that in the early years of the programme many benefits went to lower-income countries, more recent data suggest that the countries that have benefited most from preferences have been high-income developing countries with pre-existing supply capacity, and some agricultural exporters receiving high income transfers because of high non-tariff protection.

In broad terms, supply-side constraints should be distinguished from other explanations for the limited economic success of preferential trade arrangements. For example, some beneficiaries of a particular preferential scheme have largely enjoyed unrestricted access across almost the entire range of their exports. While the arrangements could doubtless be improved in various ways from the point of view of the beneficiaries, it would be difficult to point to significant obstacles to access inherent in the arrangements themselves. The only valid conclusion, therefore, is that the limited success of trade preferences in increasing the trade shares of beneficiary countries, and in fostering growth and economic diversification, must be explained primarily in terms of other constraints to development in the beneficiary countries.

The observation that preferences have made a limited contribution to economic development is not an argument for imposing obstacles upon the trade of beneficiary countries. But it does make the case against the deployment of arguments opposing multilateral trade liberalisation in the name of preserving preference margins, and for dealing with the shortcomings of the schemes.

Benefits have undoubtedly been compromised through significant restrictions, in terms of product and country coverage, and through uncertainty, the unilateral nature of the schemes, frequent changes in eligibility, complex rules of origin, and various other restrictions.[4] In fact, these are the concerns that developing countries have expressed in respect of the actual operation of the GSP schemes. In terms of products excluded from the GSP, developing countries have explicitly mentioned walnuts, raw coffee, meat, dairy products, vegetables, cereals, cigars, silk, cotton, woven fabrics of cotton and footwear. Developing countries have also expressed concern that some schemes include binding ceiling quotas on certain products where they enjoy distinct comparative advantage including wood, leather, footwear, electrical machinery and equipment. They have also pointed out that specialisation and development indices that some schemes employ can lead to discrimination between developing countries as such indices favour producers of raw materials and low-processed goods while penalising more advanced suppliers.

In the absence of such obstacles, there would have been higher utilisation ratios and greater trade benefits. But is there any reason to believe that these additional benefits would have reached much beyond the restricted group of high-income beneficiaries that captured the lion's share of what benefits there were? The only answer to this question is to better target preferences to countries that do in fact need and require them as a condition for their integration into the world economy and hence development. It is precisely because a few, relatively well-off developing countries have enjoyed most of the GSP benefits available, and at the same time have registered impressive levels of growth and development, that the need for a better targeting and tiering of benefits is called for. However, it is important to note that some developing countries remain opposed to such an approach. They have put forward the view that sector and country graduation schemes are contrary to the principles of non-discrimination and non-reciprocity that underpin the GSP. These issues are taken up in Section B below.

b. Services

Article IV of GATS foresees the participation of developing countries in the service liberalisation to be gradual, and to proceed along the developmental requirements of each member. This is to be achieved via the negotiation of specific commitments that would strengthen their domestic service capacity, efficiency and competitiveness through access to technology on commercial basis, the improvement of their access to distribution channels and information networks, and the liberalisation of market access in sectors and modes of supply of export interest to them.

Developing countries have expressed concerns over the lack of a specific mechanism to operationalise the provisions in Article IV of GATS for liberalisation of market access in sectors and modes of supply of interest to them, and the need to move ahead with implementation of Article 66.2 of the TRIPS Agreement that deals with incentives for the transfer of technology to least developed countries. As stated earlier, some developing countries have also argued that IP protection under the TRIPs Agreement is largely oriented towards areas of interest to developed countries, leaving aside areas that particularly interest them, like indigenous knowledge or geographical indications for traditional handicrafts.

(ii) Provisions to safeguard the interests of developing countries

A number of WTO Agreements provide provisions that call on members to take into account the interest of developing countries. For example, the TBT Agreement provides that in the preparation and application of technical regulations, standards and conformity assessment procedures, WTO members should aim to take into account the special development, financial and trade needs of developing countries. Similar provisions are also included in the Sanitary and Phyto-Sanitary (SPS) Agreement. The Anti-Dumping Agreement (ADA) also stipulates that constructive remedies should be explored before applying anti-dumping duties in cases where they affect the essential interests of developing countries. The Agreement on Subsidies and Countervailing Measures also stipulates the termination of countervailing duty investigations against a product originating in a developing country if the level of subsidisation or the share of imports is less than a prescribed level. A similar stipulation is also included in the Agreement on Safeguards for the non-application of safeguard measures on imports from a developing country if the import share falls below a prescribed level.

A number of developing countries have expressed the view that many such provisions have been largely ineffective. For example, where it concerns the TBT and SPS Agreements, some have complained that developed countries have not adequately taken into account their special needs in preparing and applying sanitary and phyto-sanitary measures, technical regulations, standards and conformity assessment procedures. They have also expressed concerns over a lack of initiatives to facilitate their participation in standard setting organisations.

In addition, concerning the Anti-dumping Agreement, some non-OECD countries argue that developed countries applying anti-dumping measures have paid inadequate attention to the special situation of developing countries and have not adequately explored possibilities for constructive remedies. Non-OECD countries feel that they should be accorded more flexible procedures, *e.g.* by being allowed higher *de minimis* dumping margins and import share thresholds in anti-dumping proceedings. Moreover, these countries call for a "grace period" during the initiation of proceedings, as well as special considerations when setting the investigation period.

(iii) Flexibility of commitments

Of the 145 special S&D provisions, 30 impart more flexibility to developing countries in the implementation of certain rules and commitments. For example, the Agreement on Agriculture provides a longer time-frame and lower reductions in tariffs and subsidies for developing country members; they are also not required to make commitments in respect of subsidies for marketing costs and internal transport and freight charges on export shipments during the implementation period. For non-agricultural subsidies, developing countries with per capita income less than $1000 (Annex VII countries) have been exempted from the prohibition on export subsidies as long as these do not disrupt other countries' markets. Developing countries that are not Annex VII countries have until 2003 to phase out export subsidies. There is, however, some provision for extension.

The Safeguard Agreement allows developing countries to maintain safeguard measures for a period of 10 years, instead of 8; and they may re-impose safeguard measures after half the time of a previous application in case the minimum two-year period of non-application has elapsed. The GATS also allows developing country members to open fewer sectors and liberalise fewer types of transactions while progressively extending market access in line with their level of development.

Developing countries were also given the flexibility to bind their tariffs at ceiling levels that are more often than not significantly higher than autonomously applied tariffs. In most cases, the lower applied tariffs have been introduced in the context of adjustment programmes outside the WTO reciprocal bargaining process. Thus, developing countries were given bargaining chips that they can use in future negotiations. This outcome also gave rise to the concept of "Credit for Concessions Given".

GATS Article XIX offers in addition "appropriate flexibility for individual developing countries for opening fewer sectors, liberalising fewer types of transactions, progressively extending market access in line with their developmental situation and, when making access to their markets available to foreign service suppliers, attaching to it conditions aimed at achieving the objectives referred to in Article IV."

(iv) Transitional periods

Longer time periods to facilitate implementation are provided for in all WTO agreements, save in the cases of the Agreements on the Implementation of Article VI (anti-dumping) of GATT 1994 and on Preshipment Inspection. For example, the TRIPS Agreement grants developing countries a 5 year transition period (except for the national treatment and MFN commitments), while least-developed economies are afforded up to 11 years to follow suit, with the possibility of further extensions.

Some developing countries have expressed the view that the transitional periods neither provide adequate time to deal with specific capacity constraints that many of them face, nor do they take into account their particular development needs. Specific areas in which extensions have been referred to include those related to non-agricultural export subsidies, TRIMS, TRIPS and the Customs Valuation Agreement.

(v) Technical assistance

The provision of technical assistance to developing countries has become part and parcel of S&D under the WTO Agreements. It aims at assisting developing country governments in their efforts to build institutional capacity needed to implement the Agreements and participate more fully in the multilateral trading system. This seems particularly important for implementation of SPS, TBT, Customs Valuation, GATS and TRIPS. Nevertheless, individual S&D provisions on technical assistance can be seen as "best endeavour" clauses rather than legal obligations, as they are expressed in imprecise and hortatory language.

Developing countries are asking for a substantial increase in the WTO core budget to be devoted to technical assistance programmes, and for an acceleration in the implementation of the programmes under the Integrated Framework following the submission of needs assessment by LDCs. The question of technical assistance is dealt with in more detail in Chapter VI below.

B. Tiering of S&D

Most of the concerns listed above reflect developing countries' dissatisfaction with the actual operation of a large number of S&D provisions. They consider them as inadequate instruments to help them integrate more fully into the multilateral trading system.

However, no fruitful discussion of the actual or potential contribution of S&D to integration efforts and hence economic development is complete without a full appreciation of the problems originating from the lack of an official definition of what constitutes a developing country. These problems can be illustrated by the fact that Singapore, with a per capita income of $26600 in 1998 has in principle the same access to special provisions as Ghana with a per capita income of $400. At the most basic level, no single system can pretend to address the interests and concerns of countries with such a wide difference in economic performance. Even in the unlikely event where problems and their magnitudes can be seen as more or less similar, the remedies that fit a country like Singapore must surely be different from those that Ghana could undertake. Assume for the sake of argument that even where the remedies are the same, then surely the capacity of Singapore to adopt them is different from Ghana's.

Two alternative approaches to a more differentiated treatment of developing countries can be distinguished. One approach would continue the practice initiated during the Uruguay Round of targeting more benefits to a select group of developing countries. The inevitable consequence of this approach is that the blanket special provisions under S&D would eventually become less responsive to the needs and concerns of some of the excluded countries. Thus, pressure would build to add this or that country to the list of the poorer developing countries.

The alternative approach would be to encourage the more advanced developing countries to abandon the group either on an autonomous basis, or through the elaboration of some analytical criteria for "graduation" that are based on measurable economic data. Whichever approach dominates, it is clear that multilateral co-operation in this area is of critical importance to all WTO members.

In the context of the Generalised System of Preferences (GSP), tiering contains elements from the two approaches listed above as it entails the calibration of benefits to the level of economic development achieved by a beneficiary country. Three principal tools are available for this purpose:

1. The extension of deeper benefits to those beneficiaries that are deemed to be the least-developed countries.

2. The graduation (*i.e.*, removal from GSP status) of specific products imported from beneficiaries that are deemed to be sufficiently competitive in the production of those items, and

3. The graduation of the more advanced beneficiary countries from the programme altogether.

Preference-granting countries or sponsors can use these tools to adjust the status both of countries and of products. We examine how four sponsors have employed these tools: Australia, the European Union, Japan, and the United States (Table 5.1 presents a snapshot of the key features of these programmes).

The original GSP proposal suggested that the programme as a whole lasts for just ten years, and also implied that the benefits might be reduced for the more advanced beneficiary countries (see Box 5.1). It did not directly address the question of whether individual countries might be graduated from the programme altogether. Nor was this matter clarified by the Enabling Clause, which is more properly known as the "Differential and More Favourable Treatment, Reciprocity, and Fuller Participation of

Developing Countries." This 1979 agreement granted the permanent waiver of the GSP in the GATT system. Though a preferential approach has become deeply ingrained and the principle of non-reciprocal concessions was codified in the Enabling Clause, the text of the Enabling Clause itself contains a provision to the effect that such preferential treatment should not be indefinite and should evolve through time, as developing countries state the expectation that:

> "their capacity to make contributions or negotiated concessions or take other mutually agreed action under the provisions and procedures of the General Agreement would improve with the progressive development of their economies and improvement in their trade situation and they would accordingly expect to participate more fully in the framework of rights and obligations under the General Agreement."

This formulation, which has been described as "quite vague and ambiguous,"[5] can be read in two different ways. In a narrow interpretation, the provision suggests that countries should be expected to engage more fully in the exchange of concessions as their economic development advances. A broader interpretation would hold that this clause constitutes the developing countries' acceptance of graduation as a basic principle.

Box 5.1. The origins of the GSP

The GSP was initially proposed at the first United Nations Conference on Trade and Development (UNCTAD I) in 1964 as the export-oriented complement to the "import substitution industrialisation" (ISI) model that was then in vogue among many developing countries. The original GSP proposal envisioned the extension of duty-free treatment to developing countries within a managed-trade framework. All three of the tools identified above were incorporated in the proposal:

"With regard to primary commodities and industrial goods produced by the developing countries, it is advocated that *quantitative targets* should be set for their entry into the industrial countries' market, to be reached within a specified number of years.

Within the aforesaid global value, the industrial countries could establish a quota for admitting manufactured goods from the developing countries *free of duty*, but they could *exclude from these preferences* a schedule of items constituting a reasonable percentage of the total goods they import. This exclusion could take effect from the outset or during the operation of the system, in accordance with criteria to be laid down.

Manufactures from developing countries thus excluded from the scope of preferences would be admitted by the industrial countries on the usual most-favoured-nation basis.

All the developing countries, irrespective of their level of development, would be eligible to avail themselves of the *preferential system* up to the amount of the relevant quota. But there would have to be a periodic review of the flow of exports; and if exports from one or more countries increased so much that they did not leave sufficient room for those from the others, equitable solutions should be sought.

Special preferences should be granted to the less advanced developing countries. For this purpose, the schedule of items excluded by the industrial countries from the preferential system applied to all the other developing countries should be used, where such a schedule exists."[6]

The proposed limitations on preferences were to be based not only on the need to spread around the benefits, as suggested by the above quote, but also on the idea that preferences were needed only as long as developing countries were still passing through a transitional stage. The ISI policy prevented these countries from offering "conventional reciprocity" to the industrial countries, according to the UNCTAD Secretary General's report, but in the meantime the industrial countries could benefit from the "real reciprocity" or "implicit reciprocity" stemming from the fact that developing countries "can import more than they would otherwise have been able to do had [the industrial countries'] concessions not been granted."[7] After the preferences have helped the developing countries "to prevent or rectify the structural imbalance of their trade," they "will gradually have to disappear."[8]

Box 5.1. The origins of the GSP (cont.)

Seven years passed between this original proposal and the implementation of the first GSP programmes in 1971.[9] It was necessary to build political support for the idea (which was achieved with a commitment in principle at UNCTAD II in 1968), translate the basic principles and commitments into actual agreements and programmes, and devise a legal solution to the basic incompatibility between trade preferences and the universal most-favoured-nation requirement of the General Agreement on Tariffs and Trade (GATT). The legal issues were eventually resolved through the extension of a ten-year waiver in 1971, later replaced by the permanent waiver (the Enabling Clause) in 1979.

Both UNCTAD and the OECD played important roles in this process of translating an idea into a policy. As their investigations and consultations proceeded it became increasingly apparent that it would be very difficult to create one unified system under which identical concessions would be granted across-the-board by all developed countries, because of the differences in these countries' economic structures and systems of tariff protection. The GSP thus came to be understood as a system composed of individual national schemes each based on common goals and principles and aiming to provide developing countries with broadly equivalent opportunities for expanded export growth.[10]

The first preferential imports began to enter the European Community and Japan in 1971, while the U.S. programme entered into effect in 1976. Australia converted its earlier preferential scheme into a GSP programme in 1974. Other countries implemented their programmes in 1971 (Norway), 1972 (Austria, Bulgaria, Czechoslovakia, Finland, Hungary, New Zealand, Sweden, and Switzerland), 1974 (Canada), and 1976 (Poland).

Whatever the original intent of the sponsor and beneficiary countries may have been, it is quite apparent that the graduation of countries and/or products has become a key element of the programme. All four of the schemes reviewed here provide for the graduation of countries and/or products. These two forms of graduation should be considered together, insofar as they are often closely related. Countries often are graduated in stages, such that the more advanced beneficiaries see many of their products graduated before they are removed from the programme altogether. A summary of countries' approaches to product graduations is given in Table 5.2. The results of the country graduations can be seen in Appendix 3.[11]

Graduation is most apparent in the case of the Australian programme. As a general rule, Australia has graduated (or is in the process of graduating) all countries other than the LDCs. The first step in this direction came in 1991, when Australia declared that the tariffs applied to Singapore, Chinese Taipei, Hong Kong-China, and the Republic of Korea were fixed to the July 1, 1992 rate until the general Australian tariff was reduced to that level. The margin of preferences extended to imports from these countries thus narrowed as MFN tariffs declined.

The Australian System of Tariff Preferences (ASTP) has undergone a number of changes since it was first introduced in 1966. These changes need to be seen against the progressive reform of the Australian General Tariff, with over 40% now duty-free and over 40% between 1 and 5 percent. Generally, where the General Tariff rate is equal to or greater than five percent, a five percentage points margin of preference is extended to beneficiary countries. Where the General Tariff rate is less than five percent, The ASTP is free.

Initially, the ASTP provided for non-reciprocal preferential treatment for specified manufactured and semi-manufactured goods from developing countries. Following a major review, a number of changes were introduced in 1986 with preferences extended to all dutiable goods. Since 1 July 1992, the preferential arrangements for Singapore, Taiwan, Hong-Kong China and the Republic of Korea have been phasing down. Tariffs for these countries remained fixed at the 1 July 1992 rate (5% below the General Rate) until the General Rate reduced to that level during the programme of phased reductions to the General Tariff. These countries retain duty-free status for items where the General Tariff is five percent.

In February 1993 and July 1994, arrangements were made for phasing out preferences to all but the Least Developed Countries (as defined by the UN) and certain South Pacific Island Territories. Where tariffs applied to goods from developing countries are zero or below 5 percent, or where the General Tariff rates are not phasing down, there has been no change to the preference margins for developing countries. Where tariffs for developing countries had already declined below 5% but had not reached zero, they are frozen at those levels. The five percentage points margin continues to apply where General Tariff rates are not phasing down, *e.g.* in the textiles, clothing and footwear and passenger motor vehicle sectors.

The EU used to employ a system in which GSP privileges were quantitatively limited through "fixed duty-free amounts" and "fixed reduced-duty amounts" limiting the amount of available benefits. The EU replaced this approach in 1994 with a "tariff modulation" approach that is based on tariff reductions that are differentiated according to the product's level of sensitivity. The EU also modulates the treatment extended to products and countries by providing objective standards for graduation.

The rules governing exclusion of beneficiary countries from the EU system are based on the combination of a specified level of GNP per capita and the "development index."[12] That index is designed to determine a beneficiary country's development level *vis à vis* the EU. The variables are income, population, and manufactured exports of both the beneficiary country and the EU. An index score of 0 means the development levels of the beneficiary country and the EU are equal. Income and population statistics are obtained from the World Bank while data on manufactured exports are from UNCTAD figures. The EU removed Singapore, South Korea, and Hong Kong-China from the programme in 1998, when countries that exceeded $8,210 GNP per capita (according to World Bank figures) were to be graduated if they also received a development index score greater than -1.

The graduation of products from the European Union's GSP was wholly revamped in 1994, based on sector-by-sector evaluation. According to Article 4 of the current GSP Regulation, -- the so-called "lion's share clause"-- countries whose exports to the Community of products covered by this scheme in a given sector exceeded 25% of all beneficiary countries' exports to the Community in that sector in the statistical reference year of the previous scheme" will be graduated.

On the other hand, sectors of specific beneficiary countries are graduated under the "graduation mechanism" (Article 3 of the current GSP Regulation) if the sector's specialisation index exceeds a certain threshold which depends on the country's development index. However, Article 4 part 2 states that -

> countries whose exports to the Community of products covered by the scheme in a given sector did not exceed 2% of all beneficiary countries' exports to the Community in that sector in the statistical reference year of the previous scheme shall continue to be exempt from the graduation mechanism.

Table 5.3 lists various countries that have graduated from EU GSP preferences on a product basis. The second column lists how many Harmonised Schedule chapters were partially or entirely graduated. The top three product graduates are China, Thailand, and Brazil, followed by 24 other countries with multiple product graduations.

Beneficiary countries of Japan's GSP system can graduate in three circumstances. Countries will graduate if they are classified as a "high-income economy" in the *World Bank Atlas* for three consecutive years, export more than 25 per cent of total exports to Japan, or export more than ¥1 billion in products to Japan. A country will also be graduated if it is not listed in the *Atlas* but is recognised to have the same level of GNP per capita with other "high-income economies." Nineteen countries are currently excluded from the GSP, as noted in Appendix 3.[13]

The Japanese GSP programme maintains a system of ceilings on a number of industrial products. Imports that exceed the product ceiling are subject to the general MFN rate. Ceilings play an important role in the Japanese graduation system as well. If preferential imports from a single country exceed one-fifth of the total value/quantity of the ceiling for that import, preferential treatment is suspended.

In the US, the graduation of products is governed by the competitive-need limitations (CNLs). The CNLs are intended to prevent the extension of preferential treatment to countries that are already competitive in the production of an item. The CNLs set a ceiling on GSP benefits for each product and country, and are triggered by the trade data that the GSP Subcommittee reviews on an annual basis. With certain exceptions and qualifications, a country will automatically lose its GSP eligibility for a given product the year after the CNLs are exceeded. Since 1985 there have been two CNLs in place: the original, "upper" competitive need limit and a new, "lower" limit. The "upper" CNL remains the most common, and applies to the great majority of products and countries. It is triggered on a product if during any calendar year US imports from a country account for half or more of the value of total US imports of that product or exceed a certain dollar value that is adjusted annually.[14] The figure was originally set at $25 million in 1975, and rose to $95 million by 2000. It will go up by an additional $5 million in each subsequent year (*i.e.*, it will be $100 million in 2001, $105 million in 2002, etc.). Products that have been found by the GSP Subcommittee to be "sufficiently competitive" when imported from a specified beneficiary are subject to the "lower" CNL. For these products the trigger is 25% or a dollar value set at approximately 40% of the "upper" competitive need level. The US programme also allows for temporary or permanent waivers of the CNLs for specific products, and the CNLs are automatically waived for LDCs.

The US law also provides that a beneficiary country can be graduated completely from the programme if "the President determines that a beneficiary developing country has become a 'high income' country, as defined by the official statistics of the International Bank for Reconstruction and Development." This provision has been used to graduate several Asian newly industrialised economies, among others. In addition to graduating Hong Kong-China, Korea, Singapore, and Chinese Taipei in 1989, as well as Malaysia in 1997, the United States removed Mexico from the programme when the North American Free Trade Agreement entered into effect in 1994 (Appendix 3 lists the countries that have been graduated from the programme, or have otherwise seen their preferences suspended or terminated).

(i) Subjective adjustment of privileges

Not all removals of countries and products have been made solely on the basis of objective considerations of economic development and competitiveness. Sponsor countries can use these privileges to exert influence on the beneficiary countries. For at least two of the schemes reviewed here, the sponsors have used either positive inducements (*i.e.*, expanded benefits) or negative sanctions (*i.e.*, the removal of countries or products) as a means of inducing changes in the policies of beneficiary countries.

The beneficiaries of the GSP do not have a legally enforceable right to these preferences, which are not "bound" in the sponsors' tariff commitments. It is within the authority of those sponsors to adjust the privileges that they extend to the beneficiaries. This aspect of the programme is due to the fact that the GSP is fundamentally inconsistent with the core GATT rule of non-discriminatory treatment, and thus required a waiver of GATT Article I. The GATT Contracting Parties granted a ten-year exception in 1971, and later made this waiver permanent in the 1979 Enabling Clause. This product of the Tokyo Round allowed the GATT Contracting Parties to "accord differential and more favourable treatment to developing countries, without according such treatment to other Contracting Parties." The Enabling Clause also isolated the GSP from the scope of GATT rules. This meant that beneficiary countries that were also Contracting Parties to GATT had no recourse to multilateral rules in any disputes regarding the implementation of the programme.

The EU provides a number of means to encourage compliance with internationally recognised environmental, labour, and drug policies. Section 4, Article 7 of the Regulation applying the 1999-2001 GSP programme outlines the "special arrangements supporting measures to combat drugs." This incentive is meant to reward Central and South American countries for their domestic efforts to combat drugs. Customs duties are suspended entirely for a wide range of industrial products. Notable exceptions are parts and accessories of arms and ammunitions and various sensitive agricultural products. Countries benefiting from this special arrangement are the Andean Community[15] and Central American Common Market[16] members.

Title II of the same document enumerates the EU's "special incentive arrangements concerning labour rights and environmental protection." Environmental incentives apply only to a handful of tropical forest products such as cashew apples (HS 0813.40.70) and a variety of tropical wooden products. These tariff reductions range from 90% to 65%.

The same tariff cuts are available for a variety of products to any GSP beneficiary (including LDCs) provided that:

> The authorities of those countries have applied to the Commission in writing to take advantage of the special arrangements for their originating products, giving details of:
>
> – their domestic legislation incorporating the substance of the standards laid down in ILO Conventions No 87 and No 98 concerning application of the principles of the right to organise and to bargain collectively and Convention No 138 concerning the minimum age of admission to employment; the full text of such legislation must be attached, together with an official translation into one of the Community languages,
>
> – the measures taken to apply and monitor these provisions effectively, any sectoral restrictions on their application, any breaches observed and a breakdown of such breaches by production sector,
>
> – a commitment by the government of the country in question to take full responsibility for monitoring application of the special arrangements and the relevant administrative co-operation procedures.[17]

In addition to rewarding beneficiaries for their acceptable policies, the European Union also provides for reduced benefits for countries that do not comply with certain standards. Section 1 of Title III outlines the possible scenarios for temporary withdrawal of preferences. These include:

- practice of any form of slavery or forced labour as defined in the Geneva Conventions of 25 September 1926 and 7 September 1956 and International Labour Organisation Conventions No 29 and No 105;

- export of goods made by prison labour;

- manifest shortcomings in customs controls on export or transit of drugs (illicit substances or precursors), or failure to comply with international conventions on money laundering;

- fraud or failure to provide administrative co-operation as required for the verification of certificates of origin form A;

- in manifest cases of unfair trading practices on the part of a beneficiary country. The withdrawal shall be in full compliance with the WTO rules;

- manifest cases of infringement of the objectives of international conventions such as NAFO, NEAFC, ICCAT and NASCO concerning the conservation and management of fishery resources.[18]

The 1997 temporary removal of Myanmar from the EU list of beneficiaries, a policy still in force today, was a result of this title.

In the US, the "designation criteria" that the President employs in deciding whether any specific country would be granted benefits also provide the means by which a country can be removed. A country's benefits can be reduced, suspended, or terminated if it is found not to comply with these criteria. The US policy on this matter took a new turn with the Trade and Tariff Act of 1984, which — in addition to re-authorising the GSP - made three important changes in the programme.[19] First, the designation criteria for the GSP were expanded to cover additional items (*e.g.*, labour rights). Second, the law provided for a "general review" that could lead to increases or reductions in countries' benefits. Third, the law allowed the Office of the U.S. Trade Representative (USTR) to offer countries more secure benefits by waiving the limits on GSP benefits. The USTR used these provisions in a general review of the GSP in 1985-1987, and continued to use them in subsequent annual reviews. The general review allowed interested parties (*e.g.*, firms, labour unions, interest groups, etc.) to bring complaints regarding country practices, including trade issues such as alleged restrictions on market access or failure to protect intellectual property rights. The issues raised in these petitions were discussed in the consultations that US trade officials conducted with beneficiary countries in 1986. These practices have been continued in annual reviews of the GSP.

The workers' rights criterion has been the single most common issue cited in the petitions filed with the GSP Subcommittee. Of the 224 country practices petitions that were filed with the USTR during 1985-2000, 128 concerned workers' rights.[20] Failure to meet this criterion has led to the temporary or permanent suspension of GSP privileges for Chile, Maldives, Mauritania, Paraguay, Sudan, and Syria, and their termination for Liberia, Nicaragua, and Romania. Other common topics of complaint in annual reviews concern expropriation disputes (which led to the suspension of Ethiopia's benefits during 1980-1993), intellectual property rights, and market-access issues.

The protection of intellectual property rights is among the most important designation criteria. The United States demonstrated the potential use of GSP privileges in trade disputes when in 1997 "the U.S. Government announced the suspension of 50 per cent of Argentina's GSP benefits effective in April 1997 because of Argentina's lack of patent protection for pharmaceuticals."[21]

The benefits extended to countries can also be modified as a result of other policy considerations, such as the extension of more preferential treatment to favoured trading partners. On three occasions, US officials have conducted special reviews of the GSP to grant speedy and favourable treatment to the petitions submitted by partners from specific regions. The United States conducted special reviews for Andean countries in 1989-1990, Eastern European countries in 1991-1992, and sub-Saharan African countries in 1997. In the last case, only the LDCs can receive duty-free treatment for the newly designated items.[22]

Table 5.1. **Key features of four countries' GSP programmes**

	Australian programme	*EU programme*	*Japanese programme*	*U.S. programme*
Country coverage	Restricted to UN list of forty-three least-developed countries.	Similar composition to the United States. Notable inclusions are: Mexico, China, Cuba, Iraq, Iran, Kuwait, Saudi Arabia, Malaysia, and Afghanistan. Forty-eight countries receive least-developed country treatment.	Similar to both the European Union and the United States, includes the Federal Republic of Yugoslavia, the West Bank and Gaza Strip, Cuba, Iran and Iraq. Forty-two countries receive least-developed country treatment.	Most developing countries are eligible, and many transition economies have been eligible since the end of the Cold War. Major exceptions include Mexico, China, Asian NIEs, and most OPEC members. Thirty-three countries receive least-developed country treatment.
Designation requirements	Must be on the UN's list of least-developed countries.	Unknown	Beneficiaries must be prescribed by a Cabinet Order as an appropriate country or territory for the GSP, be a member of UNCTAD, have its own tariff and trade regime, desire to receive preferences and be in a stage of development.	The law establishes some mandatory criteria (e.g., Communist countries are generally ineligible), others that are mandatory but can be waived (e.g., the country cannot expropriate U.S. investments), and still others that the president must take into account (e.g., protection of intellectual property).
Depth of tariff cuts	5% margin of preference, ASTP rate is zero if MFN rate is less than 5%, duty free access for certain handmade goods.	15%-100% tariff cuts on GSP-designated products.	Minimum unknown-100% tariff cuts on GSP-designated products.	100% tariff cuts on GSP-designated products.
Removal of products	No traditional graduation system.	Based on the combination of two indices: a) a development index that compares several economic indicators of the beneficiary and the European Union; and b)	Ceilings system sets a quota for several industrial, GSP-eligible products. Once quota is reached, beneficiaries must pay MFN rates. If preferential imports from one country exceed one-fourth of the ceiling, preferences may be suspended for that country.	"Competitive-need" limits generally lead to loss of GSP for an item when a country accounts for more than half of U.S. imports or a certain dollar figure ($95 million in 2000). Petitions can seek the removal of a product on either a global or country-specific basis.

(continued)

Table 5.1. **Key features of four countries' GSP programmes** (continued)

	Australian programme	*EU programme*	*Japanese programme*	*U.S. programme*
Duration	Australia created the original preferential program in 1966, well before the other OECD countries. It expanded this program and brought it under the GSP waiver in 1974.	The first two programs spanned 10 years each (1971-1981, 1981-1991). The second program was extended until the conclusion of the Uruguay Round. The program was then substantially changed for the 1995-2004 period. The current authorisation is for the period of July 1, 1999-December 31, 2001.	Effective period listed: August 1, 1971-March 31, 2001.	Originally extended for 10 years (in 1975) and then renewed for 8½ years (in 1984), the program has periodically expired and been retroactively renewed since 1993.

Table 5.2. **Product graduation programmes**

Country	**Rules and principles**
Australia	No product graduations; nearly all countries that are not LDCs have already been graduated, and LDCs enjoy GSP treatment for virtually all imports.
Japan	Ceilings on various industrial products regulate the amount that may enter under preferences. These operate like a tariff-rate quota: Once a ceiling is reached, products enter under the MFN rate. Countries that export more than 25 percent of the total value/quantity of the ceiling for that product lose preferences.
European Union	The graduation mechanism applies to countries whose exports to the EU in a sector exceed 25 percent of all beneficiary exports; it does not apply to countries whose exports did not exceed 2 percent of total beneficiary countries' exports to the EU in that sector.
United States	Products are graduated on a country-specific basis if they exceed the competitive-need limits. These are generally triggered whenever imports of a product from a country exceed either a dollar-value limit ($95 million in 2000) or half of U.S. imports of that product.

Table 5.3. **European Union product graduations**

Country	**Chapters for which beneficiary is graduated in whole or in part**
China	35
Thailand	29
Brazil	24
India	14
Pakistan	14
Malaysia	13
Argentina	12
Kazakhstan	12
Russia	11
Indonesia	7
Chile	5
Mexico	4
Ukraine	4
Belarus	3
Libya	3
Macao	3
Saudi Arabia	3
Albania	2
Armenia	2
Azerbaijan	2
Georgia	2
Moldova	2
South Africa	2
Tajikistan	2
Turkmenistan	2
Uruguay	2
Uzbekistan	2
Brunei	1
Philippines	1

Source: "Council Regulation (EC) No 2820/98 of 21 December 1998, applying a multi-annual scheme of generalised system of preferences for the period 1 July 1999 to 31 December 2001." Annex II, Part 1. *Official Journal of the European Communities.* L357, Volume 41, December 30, 1998. Office for Official Publications of the European Communities: Luxembourg, pages 73-78.

Notes

1 Membership in the WTO as of 30 November 2000.

2 However, other members can challenge the self-proclamation as a developing country. In fact, this was the case in specific areas such as in respect of intellectual property. This challenge can then lead to negotiations to clarify the position. For countries that have negotiated to join the WTO after 1995, their status is a matter taken up during accession negotiations.

3 The 145 S&D provisions are spread across the different Multilateral Agreements on Trade in Goods; GATS; TRIPS; the Understanding on Rules and Procedures governing the Settlement of Disputes; and various Ministerial Decisions. Of the 145 provisions, 107 were adopted at the end of the Uruguay Round, and 22 apply exclusively to the least-developed WTO members (Document WT/COMTD/W/77, October 2000, WTO, Geneva).

4 Developing countries have mentioned that the linking of benefits in some schemes to non-trade objectives, such as environmental and social standards, as well as intellectual property rights and the fight against drugs curtail the benefits under the schemes and introduce elements of discrimination and reciprocity into the GSP.

5 Abdulqawi A. Yusuf, "'Differential and More Favourable Treatment': The GATT Enabling Clause," *Journal of World Trade Law* Volume 14 Number 6 (November-December, 1980), page 505.

6 United Nations Conference on Trade and Development. *Towards a New Trade Policy for Development* E/CONF.46/3 (1964), pages 143-144. Emphasis in the original.

7 *Ibid*., page 37.

8 *Ibid*., page 44.

9 Australia implemented a precursor to the GSP in 1966, just two years after UNCTAD I. It later recast the programme under the rubric of the GSP in 1974.

10 Organisation for Economic Co-operation and Development, *The Generalised System of Preferences: Review of the First Decade* (Paris: OECD, 1983), page 10.

11 It must be stressed that not all of the countries and territories shown as graduated in Appendix 3 were removed solely for reasons of their economic development. In some cases, benefits have been suspended or terminated for subjective reasons, as discussed later. The available information do not always indicate the precise reason why a country or territory that was previously eligible for the GSP is no longer included on the list of beneficiaries.

12 the EU development index is defined as $\{\log[(Y_i/POP_i)/(Y_{ue}/POP_{ue})] + \log[X_i/X_{ue}]\}/2$. Where Yi= the beneficiary country's income. Y_{ue}= the EU's income. POP_i= the beneficiary country's population. POP_{ue} =the population of the European Union. X_i = the value of the

beneficiary country's manufactured exports. X_{ue}= the value of the European Union's manufactured exports.

13 UNCTAD, *Handbook on the Scheme of Japan: 2000/2001* (Geneva: UNCTAD, 2000).

14 Certain products can obtain a waiver under section 504(d). The percentage provision is waived for items that were not produced in the United States on January 3, 1985, as provided for in Section 504(d) of the GSP law. The list can be modified through petitions submitted in an annual review. For those products on this list, a 504(d) waiver will automatically be granted when required each year.

15 Bolivia, Colombia, Ecuador, Peru, and Venezuela.

16 Costa Rica, El Salvador, Guatemala, Honduras, Nicaragua, and Panama.

17 "Council Regulation (EC) No 2820/98 of 21 December 1998 applying a multiannual scheme of generalised tariff preferences for the period 1 July 1999 to 31 December 2001." *Official Journal* L 357, 30/12/1998, page 0001-0112.

18 *Ibid.*

19 See Stephen Lande and Craig VanGrasstek, "Renewal of the Generalised System of Preferences: Neoreciprocity and the Newly Industrialised Countries." Chapter 4 of *The Trade and Tariff Act of 1984: Trade Policy in the Reagan Administration* (Lexington, Massachusetts: D.C. Heath, 1986).

20 Secretariat's calculations based on data provided by USTR.

21 Office of the U.S. Trade Representative, *1997 National Trade Estimate: Argentina*. (Washington, D.C.: U.S. Government Printing Office, 1997), page 11.

22 Both the Andean and the African reviews preceded the establishment of special programmes for those respective regions (i.e., the Andean Trade Preferences Act and the African Growth and Opportunities Act).

VI. THE CONTRIBUTION OF DEVELOPMENT CO-OPERATION

For the less advanced developing countries, benefiting from the multilateral trading system and enhancing their integration into the globalising world economy requires the pursuit of a comprehensive development strategy that would seek to create the conditions for private sector-driven development. This could be achieved through, *inter alia*, continued efforts at liberalising trade and investment regimes, building supply-side capacities, and enhancing the competitiveness of the private sector. This is by no means an easy task as it requires major efforts to help these countries strengthen their basic human and institutional capacities in the trade area.

This Chapter sets out the strategies and programmes of the donor community that aim to assist developing countries in their efforts to enhance their integration into the global economy. The fundamental objective is to ensure that their people are able to share in the benefits generated by the globalisation process. The potential benefits of enhanced integration have been quantified in a set of key development objectives that were articulated in partnership with the development community. In order to implement this ambitious multifaceted development agenda, the development community has formulated a Comprehensive Development Framework. The framework is being operationalised through country-specific poverty reduction strategies where trade reforms play a central role. In addition, capacity-building and technical assistance programmes are specifically designed so as to assist the less advanced developing countries with their integration efforts.

A. Key development objectives

In May 1996 the Development Assistance Committee of the OECD published *Shaping the 21st Century* a policy paper calling for a global partnership to pursue a new development strategy focused on a set of key development objectives to be reached by 2015 or earlier.[1] These goals are to:

- Reduce by half the proportion of people in extreme poverty.
- Achieve universal primary education in all countries and eliminate gender disparities in education.
- Reduce infant and child mortality by two-thirds and maternal mortality by three-fourths.
- Provide universal access to reproductive health services.
- Implement national strategies for sustainable development and ensure that the current loss of environmental resources is reversed.

B. The comprehensive development framework

In order to underpin these ambitious objectives, the donor community has moved towards comprehensive approaches to development strategies, as captured in the Comprehensive Development

Framework (CDF) for addressing the multifaceted development agenda.[2] The framework offers a concept for achieving greater effectiveness in the fight against poverty and the promotion of economic growth. It is based on the principle that the partner country, and not donor agencies, should determine the goals, timing, and sequencing of its development strategy, *i.e.* be its owner. Governments should build partnerships with the private sector, NGOs, donor agencies, and civil society representatives to articulate a long-term collective understanding of the needs and solutions that would generate sustained national support. Within this framework, structural and social concerns should be treated equally with macro-economic and financial ones.

The proposed framework focuses on four areas of development — structural, human, physical, and sectoral. Structural elements include honest and competent governments; strong property and personal rights laws supported by an efficient and honest legal and judicial system; a well-regulated financial system that promotes transparency; and, a strong social safety net. Human development targets include universal education and a health system that focuses on family planning and childcare. Physical concerns focus on the efficient provision of water and sewerage; access to reliable electric power; to road, rail, and air transportation and to telecommunications; preservation of the physical environment; and a commitment to preserving indigenous cultures and values. Sectoral elements include an integrated rural development strategy, a strong urban management approach, and an enabling environment for the private sector.

A stable macro-economy, shaped by prudent fiscal and monetary policies, is an essential complement to the development efforts the CDF proposes. The framework aims to allow strategic thinking about the sequencing of policies, programmes and projects, through fostering transparency when trade-offs are necessary between the macroeconomic and social objectives. Trade reforms are an integral part of the CDF. They seek to ensure that trade policy priorities are set according to the development stage of each country, and are consistent with reform efforts in other areas such as exchange rate policies, foreign direct investment, competition and labour practices. The priority each country accords to trade issues are thus dependent on the conditions specific to the economy and should come about through a national dialogue revolving around development priorities and appropriate responses. Consequently, the way the principles are put into practice will vary from country to country, depending on economic and social needs and the priorities of partner countries.

C. Poverty reduction strategies

Recently, the development community has made poverty reduction a more central and explicit goal in the context of its support to poorer partner countries. Based on the Comprehensive Development Framework, this focus has led to the introduction of comprehensive, country-owned Poverty Reduction Strategy Papers (PRSPs).

The PRSP process has made the formulation and implementation of trade reform policies more challenging, but also more enduring, in at least three respects. First, transitory adverse consequences that planned trade reforms may have on the poor groups will have to be made explicit in order to design appropriate policies to offset them. In some cases, consideration of the distribution of adjustment costs could lead to rethinking the timing and sequencing of reforms. Second, the PRSP is envisaged to be the result of a participatory process, which should strengthen the sense of ownership of the policies by the authorities and the public. This is particularly significant in the context of trade reforms, because it will on the one hand help counter affected interest groups' resistance, and, on the other support the implementation of agreed policies. Third, the PRSP process includes systematic monitoring of changes in poverty outcomes over time, as well as evaluation of the impact of key policies that can be used to inform the ongoing dialogue about the impact of trade reforms on different groups in the society.

In supporting trade reforms in the context of PRSPs, donor programmes will continue to emphasise the adoption of sound macroeconomic policies and complementary structural reforms aimed at developing competitive markets. An appropriate macroeconomic environment remains an essential condition for outward-oriented national trade policies. Trade policy reforms in the PRPS context would typically include the elimination of quantitative restrictions, state trading monopolies, preferential treatment and other NTBs on imports; the removal of export subsidies and controls; and an appropriate movement toward broadly uniform and reasonably low tariffs. In this regard, it would also be important to ensure that any revenue losses associated with tariff reduction are compensated for by the introduction of less distortionary broad-based domestic taxes. In addition, reforms will aim at substantially improving tax and customs administration and scaling back administrative discretion in granting tax and tariff exemptions and other favourable treatment to select groups. Aside from their direct impact on improving the efficiency and performance of the trade sector and, in turn, on spurring economic growth, such policy reforms contribute substantially to enhanced transparency and improved governance.

D. Building capacities for trade

There are currently major technical assistance efforts being carried out involving bilateral and multilateral aid agencies, including the *Integrated Plan of Action for the Least-Developed Countries* that is supported by a partnership between the WTO, UNCTAD and ITC Secretariats and in collaboration with the staff of the IMF, the World Bank and UNDP. Together, these organisations have developed a comprehensive and integrated framework for the provision of technical assistance to the LDCs. The framework includes initiatives to build infrastructure, streamline the business environment, ensure the efficiency and transparency of customs administration, increase government capacity to develop effective trade policies, and enhance the private sector's ability to identify and operate in export markets. The World Bank has in addition initiated programmes (particularly in favour of the least developed countries) where implementation of WTO agreements has become an integral part of development projects.

The *Integrated Framework* has been applied on a case-by-case basis to meet the development needs identified by individual LDCs through round-table meetings with donors and international agencies. This approach was endorsed by the High-Level Meeting on *Integrated Initiatives for Least-Developed Countries' Trade Development*, organised by the WTO in October 1997 and extended beyond the six original organisations to involve many aid agencies, multilateral, regional and national. However, the mandated review of the *Integrated Framework* pointed to some shortcomings related to unclear definition of policy objectives, weak administration and co-ordination as well as lack of monitoring capability. Subsequently, the six core agencies agreed to make every effort to "support the integration of trade, trade-related technical assistance and capacity building into the national development strategies and plans of LDCs," with more financial support from donor countries (WT/LDC/SEG/IF/2, 12 July 2000). In this context, one important question to be explored by WTO members is whether or not to link the binding of technical assistance commitments to specific liberalisation commitments to be implemented by LDCs.

The Integrated Framework is a significant undertaking for at least two reasons: first, WTO members have come to recognise that despite major efforts at trade reform, several poor countries still face a wide range of supply side constraints which prevent them from reaping the full benefits from the multilateral trading system. And, second, given the enormous challenges facing some of the poorer developing countries and the limited resources available, co-ordinated, integrated and demand-led responses are critical to the effectiveness of donor support. Where the Integrated Framework has fallen short is particularly in the implementation process at the country level.

E. The scope of the agenda

In collaboration with the international community, bilateral donors can play a potentially important role in responding effectively to the wide range of needs of partner countries. Their contributions could usefully focus on helping to (i) formulate and implement policies at both the national and international levels; and (ii) promote competitiveness in general.

The starting point for formulating and implementing national and international policies to effectively join the globalisation process will be the articulation of clear national objectives as a key component of a comprehensive development strategy. Such objectives must be anchored in a national consensus supported by the private sector and civil society in order to sustain the reform process.

The strategy must also include agendas for building the human resource and institutional capacities of the public sector with a view of helping countries:

- Put in place a trade-friendly policy environment including liberalisation of trade policies; legal and regulatory framework and rule of law; rationalisation and simplification of customs and administrative procedures affecting trade; an efficient physical and telecommunications infrastructure (such as through privatisation and deregulation of monopolies).

- Analyse and monitor multilateral and regional trade issues, formulating and implementing coherent trade policies, and participating effectively in international and regional negotiations; and

- Implement international and regional trading agreements.

Promoting competitiveness includes building the human resource and institutional capacity for the private sector and its associations to:

- Analyse and monitor trade issues, articulate the concerns of the private sector in the trade policy process and meet the requirements imposed by the international trading system, such as through improved access to information and the capacity to adjust to stringent environmental, food and other standards;

- Bring entrepreneurs into regional and global markets through such instruments as regional co-operation and integration, private sector networks and clusters, and expanded use of e-commerce.

F. Promoting effective partnerships

Bilateral donors can add significant value to the implementation of integrated approaches. They have the benefit of decades of experience in project implementation and evaluation, a strong field presence and well-established dialogues with the private sector and civil society in many partner countries. Ways to improve partnership approaches to capacity development for trade include the following:

- Acquiring knowledge of trade policy. Bilateral agencies must have a basic understanding of the role of trade in the development process in general, and of trade policy issues more specifically.

Regular dialogues between the trade and development communities will help to develop a common understanding and improve the quality of approaches to build capacity for trade.

- Tailoring donor responses to partner country's needs. Needs assessments undertaken by the partner country must be the starting point for any donor response. Domestic participatory consultations with a wide range of domestic actors will be a critical element in the process of identifying these needs. This is essential for ownership and sustainability. All key stakeholders from the public and private sectors, from academic research institutions and civil society, must be engaged throughout the process. If the process is truly participatory, that in itself will build capacity through the exchange of ideas and the knowledge sharing that takes place. However, trade-related needs must, in particular, be identified through the lens of the business sector to ensure that capacity development for trade is ultimately driven by the private sector.

- Assessing needs in the context of a development strategy. Donor responses must be based on realistic needs appraisal and assessments of what can be achieved under prevailing local conditions. Capacity development cannot be realised with quick fixes but has to take place in a gradual and evolutionary manner. In order to be coherent, trade needs to be better integrated into a comprehensive country strategy in co-operation with both multilateral and bilateral agencies.

- Ensuring coherence among the trade and aid communities. The division of responsibilities among ministries for trade and trade-related policy formulation runs the risk of incoherent policies if adequate consultation mechanisms are lacking. This might be further aggravated by the fact that donors operate through different channels. In the context of the Integrated Framework, for instance, the focal point has been the Ministries of Trade, Commerce and Tourism rather than the traditional agencies that deal with foreign assistance such as Ministries of Finance, Planning or Development. Donors can help create consultative mechanisms for trade policy making to resolve this problem.

- Fostering co-operation mechanisms among donor agencies. Given the magnitude of the trade-related challenges, the scarcity of aid resources, and the importance of avoiding duplication, there is a clear need for donor co-operation, co-ordination and a practical division of labour. No single donor can possibly respond effectively to the diverse range of developing country needs. This co-ordination must ultimately be partner-driven. Aid co-ordination activities, such as Consultative Group or Roundtables in partner countries, provide effective opportunities for strengthening country ownership and enabling stronger government leadership, as well as greater scope for engaging domestic stakeholders and disseminating information.

- Fostering coherent donor approaches. Evidence seems to suggest that specific trade objectives of donors may sometimes clash with their development objectives. For instance, trade-related assistance to developing countries may be focussed on the liberalisation of import regimes, with relatively less assistance directed towards improving the capacity to challenge measures that adversely affect donors' own exports. Donors must therefore take steps to ensure neutrality of their support.

NOTES

1 OECD/DAC (1996) Shaping the 21st Century: The Contribution of Development Co-operation.

2 See Comprehensive Development Framework, Country experiences, World bank, September 2000.

VII. CONCLUDING REMARKS

Once one moves beyond the bounds of autarky, every economy ultimately depends on the world economy as the arbiter of economic value; goods and services are worth no more and no less than the prices at which they can be obtained from or provided to the world market. Thus, an economy that admits relatively undistorted signals about world scarcity and permits actors to respond to them is ultimately likely to do a very much better job of creating and preserving value and wealth than one which does not.

It is also the case that even the closest managers of an economy cannot consider every detail, whereas, as Adam Smith noted, a community of individuals each responding to self-interest informed by market signals can more or less do so. Governments cannot prevent individuals from making the best of their own particular circumstances (as behaviour under, say, the Soviet system demonstrated), so the key to success is to harness this huge motive force to the right set of signals. This is what market forces do. Subject to the correction of obvious market failures such as missing markets, externalities and public goods, market forces encourage economic actors to respond flexibly to the incentives they perceive around them.

This is what openness offers: the creation and preservation of value and wealth, and a much more reliable way to develop constructive responses to challenges than bureaucratic centralism. This was not lost on the big economic powers who, over fifty years ago, realised that reducing barriers to the international flows of goods and services was vital to economic recovery from the Great Depression. They set up the General Agreement on Tariffs and Trade (GATT) whose most important function is to serve as a forum for multilateral trade negotiations (MTNs). So far, GATT has organised a total of eight rounds of MTNs, the last of which was the Uruguay Round (1986-1994) which led to the creation of the WTO. The eight rounds have been the major contributory factor behind the freeing of markets, and the increased cross-borders flows of goods and services. And the establishment of the WTO in 1995 has greatly strengthened the permanent institutional mechanisms for the discussion of trade issues and the resolution of disputes.

The WTO serves many other functions too. It facilitates domestic reforms and improves access to export markets; it fosters the adoption of good domestic policies by guaranteeing against policy reversal and by making promises of future reforms credible; and it helps countries defend their market access rights.

Completion of the Uruguay Round of trade negotiations has resulted in broad based tariff reductions and the easing of some of the important non-tariff barriers, greatly enhancing the prospects for reaping global welfare gains from further trade expansion. However, market access still represents perhaps the single most important trading issue between OECD and non-OECD countries. Market access barriers to agriculture and some labour-intensive exports from non-OECD countries continue to constrain these countries' export performance. In the area of agriculture, high tariffs, quotas and subsidies limit the ability of non-OECD countries, especially the poorest amongst them, to expand their production base into more processed, higher value-added and faster growing products. Escalating tariffs against exports of some sensitive industrial products have the same effect. A full development of trade links between OECD and non-OECD countries requires progress in reducing remaining trade restrictions, especially on product categories where non-OECD countries enjoy a comparative advantage.

It also requires providing adequate responses to concerns raised by a number of (WTO self-elected) developing countries over the operation of some of the agreements. They cite excessively burdensome implementation problems in some areas. These problems are compounded by complaints over OECD countries' efforts at integrating quotas under the MFA, and a perception that special and differential treatment provisions accorded to them no longer respond to their trading interests in a post-Uruguay Round environment.

Where matters concern special and differential treatment, the study distinguishes two alternative approaches: one approach would continue the practice initiated during the Uruguay Round of targeting more benefits to a select group of developing countries. The inevitable consequence of this approach is that the blanket special provisions under S&D would eventually become less responsive to the needs and concerns of some of the excluded countries. Thus, pressure would build to add this or that country to the list of the poorer developing countries. The alternative approach would be to encourage the more advanced developing countries to abandon the group either on an autonomous basis, or to develop some analytical criteria for "graduation" that are based on measurable economic data. Whichever approach dominates, it is clear that multilateral co-operation in this area is of critical importance to all WTO members.

Ensuring that the WTO can work more effectively to the benefit of all its members is a responsibility for all to share. While this study has focused almost exclusively on the role of OECD countries in helping other countries to fully realise their export potential, it is also important to note that some non-OECD countries could also consider how best to contribute to these efforts. Specifically, in some relatively well-off "developing countries," especially among those that have been enjoying the benefits of open trade, and at the same time have registered impressive levels of growth and development, there is still great scope for expansion of trade by poor countries. For example, during the period 1996-98, the annual average exports of all 48 least-developed countries were scarcely more than $22.7 billion, of which $17 billion was exported to the Quad (Canada, EU, Japan and the US). The rest of the world took in a mere $5.7 billion of LDC exports.

A corollary of seeking a more differentiated treatment of developing countries is the need to recognise the crucial importance of development co-operation for poorer countries. The study argues that for the less advanced developing countries, benefiting from the multilateral trading system and enhancing their integration into the globalising world economy requires the pursuit of a comprehensive development strategy that would seek to create the conditions for private sector-driven development. This could be achieved through, *inter alia*, continued efforts at liberalising trade and investment regimes, building supply-side capacities, and enhancing the competitiveness of the private sector. This is by no means an easy task as it requires major efforts to help these countries strengthen their basic human and institutional capacities in the trade area. The study then sets out the strategies and programmes of the donor community that aim to assist non-OECD countries in their efforts to enhance their integration into the global economy. The fundamental objective is to ensure that their people are able to share in the benefits generated by the globalisation process.

APPENDIX 1. LABOUR STANDARDS AND THE WTO

In December 1996, Trade Ministers issued a Declaration on core labour standards at the First WTO Ministerial Meeting, held in Singapore (WTO, 1996):

> "We renew our commitment to the observance of internationally recognised core labour standards. The International Labour Organisation (ILO) is the competent body to set and deal with these standards, and we affirm our support for its work in promoting them. We believe that economic growth and development fostered by increased trade and further trade liberalisation contribute to the promotion of these standards. We reject the use of labour standards for protectionist purposes, and agree that the comparative advantage of countries, particularly low-wage developing countries, must in no way be put into question. In this regard, we note that the WTO and ILO Secretariats will continue their existing collaboration."

Repeated references have been made since then to this Ministerial statement of support for the ILO as the competent body to set and deal with core labour standards.

In preparing their inputs for the Third WTO Ministerial Declaration for Seattle in December 1999, the US, the EU and Canada submitted proposals to address trade and labour questions. The US proposed the establishment of a Working Group on Trade and Labour, to operate under the supervision of the WTO General Council (WTO, 1999a). The European Communities proposed that the Third WTO Ministerial adopt a decision to establish a joint ILO/WTO Standing Working Forum on trade, globalisation and labour issues (WTO, 1999b). Canada proposed the establishment of a WTO working group to report to the next Ministerial Conference on the relationships between appropriate trade, developmental, social and environmental policy choices in the context of the experiences of and challenges faced by all WTO members in adjusting to globalisation (WTO, 1999c).

These proposals were discussed in Seattle and attracted opposition from a number of WTO Members. Reactions in Seattle were particularly strong against suggestions for the use of trade sanctions against those who violate core labour standards. In view of the fact that no Ministerial Declaration was concluded, the future of the proposals to set up working groups appears uncertain. Another suggestion made by the future head of the WTO would involve a high-level dialogue convened by a 'neutral' institution such as UNCTAD or ECOSOC reviewing the relationship between labour standards and the trading system, including the question of social safety nets.

Matters relevant to labour standards have also been raised routinely by a few OECD Member countries in the course of the reviews in the WTO Trade Policy Review Body (TPRB). On the other hand, developing country participants in the TPRB have repeatedly expressed the view that issues relating to core labour standards should be raised in the ILO rather than the WTO. In October 1999 in its Report to the WTO Ministerial, the TPRB reconfirmed the objectives and coverage of the Trade Policy Review Mechanism, set out in Annex 3 of the Marrakech Agreement.

APPENDIX 2. THE LEAST DEVELOPED COUNTRIES IN WORLD TRADE

The United Nations has designated 48 countries, with a total population of more than 610 million, as least developed countries (LDCs).[1] LDCs are the weakest partners in the international community with important structural problems, often compounded by natural or human-invoked disasters. They face many difficulties in their efforts to develop both human and economic capital. These include structural rigidities, low skill capacity, poor infrastructure, weak institutions and a private sector stifled by parastatals, and overwhelming debt burdens.[2] The combination of these and other problems led to a decline of 0.1 percent in LDCs' real per capita GDP during the period 1980-90. Similarly, during the same period, LDCs' share in global exports fell from 0.8 to 0.4 percent - a decline implying average annual export earning losses of $7 billion, an amount which could have wiped out a full 60 percent of their total 1990 external debt. Despite a relatively better economic performance during the period 1991-1997 when real per capita incomes grew by an average of 0.5 percent, their share in global exports remained at 0.4 percent throughout the period.

Small and declining share in world trade

Trade accounts for a very small percentage of GDPs in most LDCs compared to other developing countries, and has shown very sluggish growth. Exports contribute some 8 percent to GDP in LDCs versus 26 percent in all developing countries, and have shown growth half that of developing countries' export growth since 1980. Imports to LDCs are also small (15 percent of GDP versus 27 percent for all developing countries), and growth has been equally slow. These low growth levels are all the more dramatic against a backdrop of very low GDP growth (less than 2 percent annually since 1980, compared to 3.5 percent for all developing countries) and negative real GDP growth per capita for many of them.

The participation of LDCs in international trade remains insignificant (Appendix Figure 1). In 1998, the total value of their exports amounted to $ 21.7 billion - which was less than what Portugal alone exported during that same year. This represented only 0.4 percent of world exports and 1.4 percent of all developing countries' exports. The single largest product group was mineral fuels (25 percent) followed by manufactured goods (20 percent) composed mainly of textiles and clothing products. Food and live animals products made up the third largest product group (18%), followed by crude materials (16%) and miscellaneous manufactured products (15%) which included mainly footwear and other fabrics products. On the import side, LDCs' total import bill amounted to $ 31.7 billion in 1998 which represents 0.6 percent of total world imports, and 1.7 percent of all developing countries' imports.

1 Afghanistan, Angola, Bangladesh, Benin, Bhutan, Burkina Faso, Burundi, Cambodia, Cape Verde, Central African Republic, Chad, Comoros, Congo (ex-Zaire), Djibouti, Equatorial Guinea, Eritrea, Ethiopia, Gambia, Guinea, Guinea Bissau, Haiti, Kiribati, Laos, Lesotho, Liberia, Madagascar, Malawi, Maldives, Mali, Mauritania, Mozambique, Myanmar, Nepal, Niger, Rwanda, Samoa, Sao Tome and Principe, Sierra Leone, Solomon Islands, Somalia, Sudan, Tanzania, Togo, Tuvalu, Uganda, Vanuatu, Yemen, Zambia.

2 In 1997, the total debt of LDCs stood at US$ 127 billion up from US$ 71 billions in 1985. The ratio of total debt to GDP in 1997 was 79 percent, and its servicing consumed 13 percent of these countries' export earnings in 1997.

Equally important, LDCs' share in world trade has been declining since 1980 (Appendix Figure 2). Several factors may help explain this trend: high export commodity concentration coupled with volatile commodity markets; pricing practices in the international markets for commodities; declining share of raw materials in world trade; the small and sluggish manufacturing sector in most LDCs; and last, the structure of trade barriers facing LDCs' exports in their major markets.

Appendix Figure 1. LDC participation in world trade, 1998 (in million US)

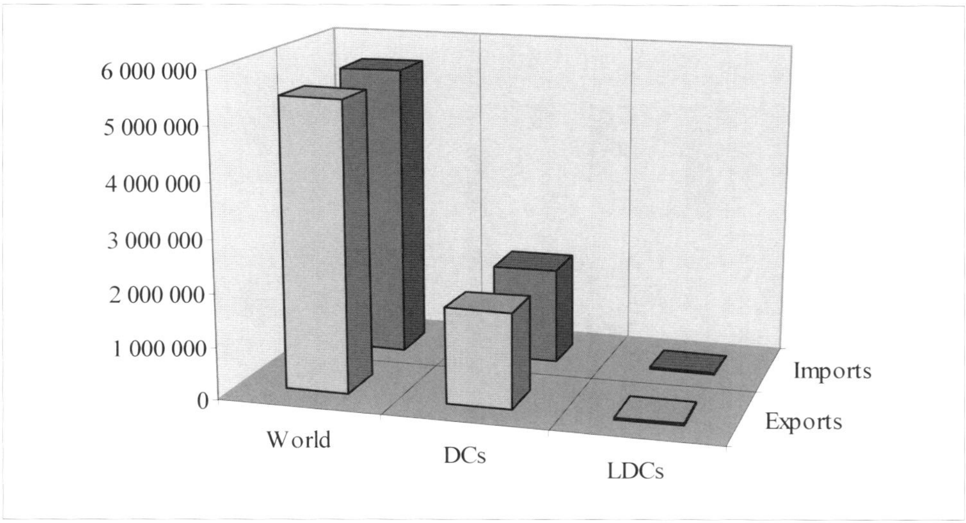

Source : UNCTAD, *Trade and Development Report.*

Appendix Figure 2. The declining share of LDC exports in world exports, 1980-1998

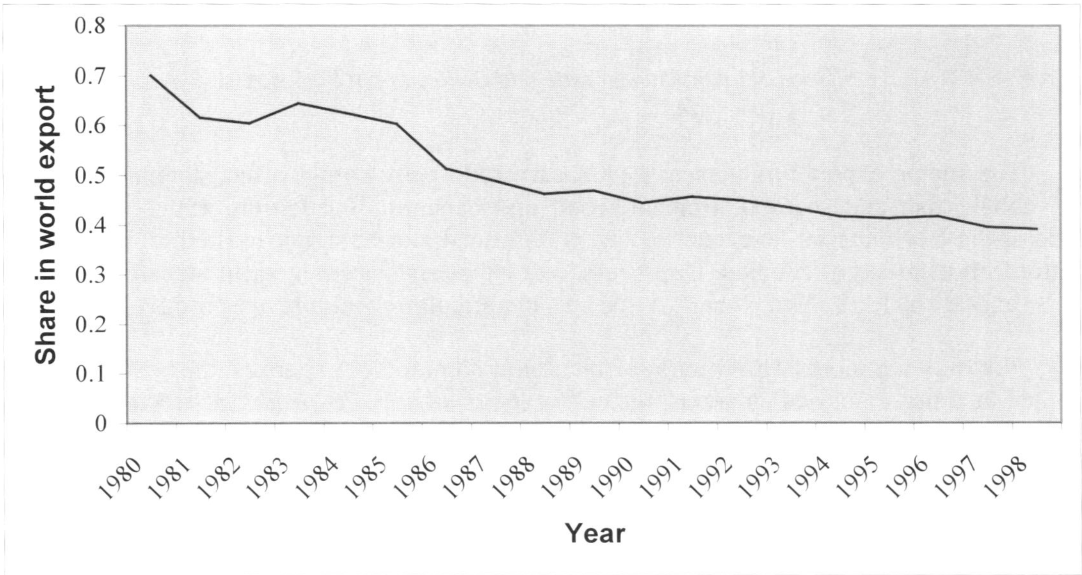

Source : UNCTAD, *Trade and Development Report.*

In addition to LDCs' meagre share in world trade, they generally export a small number of commodities. On average, a typical LDC exports some 230 commodities as opposed to 1937 products exported by Greece, for example, or 2405 for Mexico.[3] The majority of LDCs' exports are concentrated in just two or three products. On average, the top three export commodities account for close to 70 percent of total exports in each of the 48 countries (Appendix Figure 3).

Appendix Figure 3. Dependence on top 3 export products

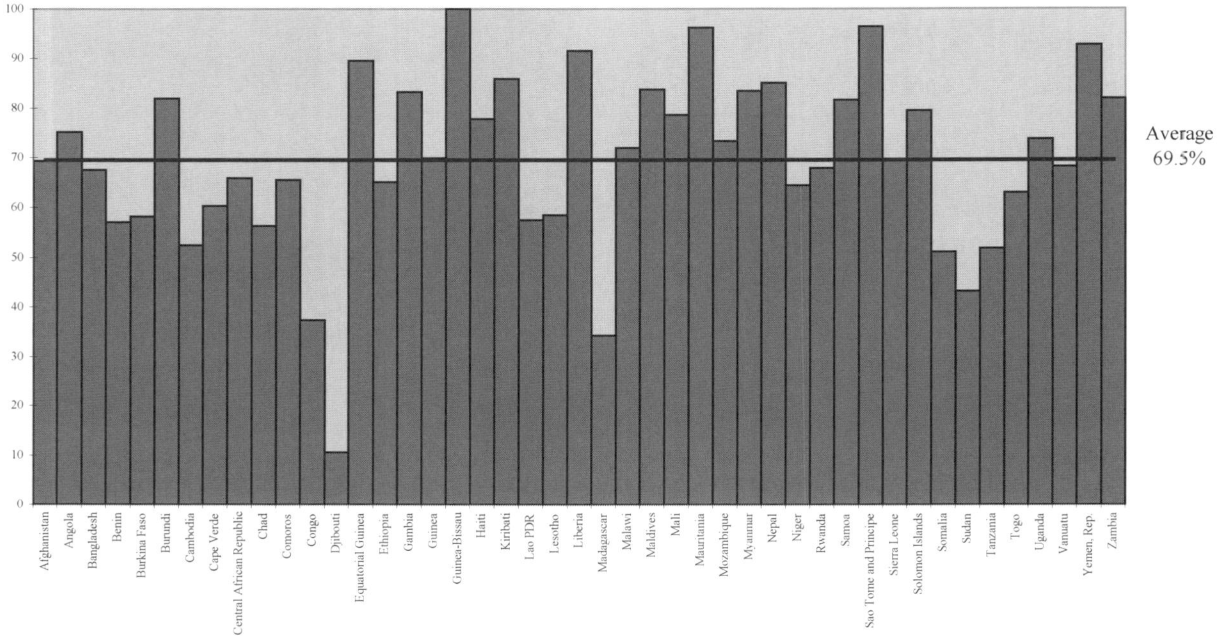

Source : UNCTAD, *Handbook of International Trade and Development Statistics*

The major export products of LDCs are crude petroleum, coffee, diamonds, cotton, jute, copper, cobalt, fish and seafood, tropical wood and bananas. In addition, almost all products are exported at the raw material level: petroleum is unrefined, coffee is not roasted, diamonds are uncut and cotton is not carded or combed. Unprocessed raw materials accounted for an estimated 75 percent of LDCs' exports in 1998. Almost half of this was in agriculture and forestry products.

Not only are most LDCs mono- or bicultural commodity exporters, they often compete with each other in other countries' markets. Indeed, exports of just *20 products account for almost 70 percent of total exports of LDCs taken together.*

3 Exports at the SITC five digit product level of a minimum of 10,000 US dollars. Data at the product level used in this study are in fact mirror data, i.e., imports from LDCs by all OECD Member countries and 12 major non-OECD importers. Analysis here is based on import data from 47 LDCs excluding Lesotho for which reliable data are not available.

Volatile commodity markets

Exporting largely raw materials, LDCs are particularly affected by changes in volatile commodity markets. For example, when the world price of cotton fell by one-third of its value between 1990 and 1992, Benin, Chad and Mali lost one quarter of their total export earnings due solely to *price volatility* (Appendix Figure 4). Prices of some agricultural commodities, particularly cotton and coffee, were high in 1995 and have since fallen. Export earnings since 1998 may therefore be even less favourable to LDCs than is suggested here.

Appendix Figure 4. Composite commodity prices facing LDCs

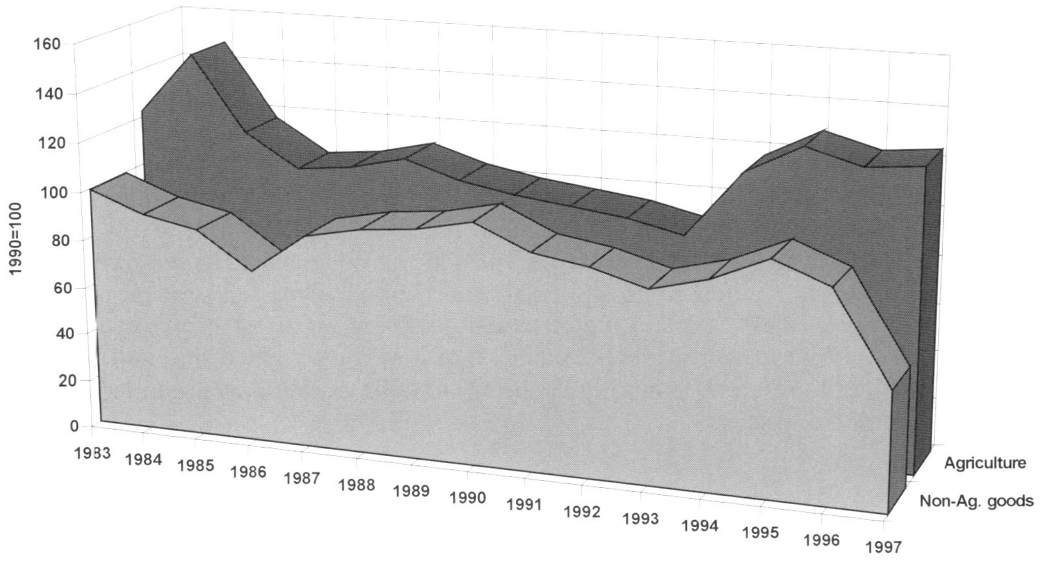

Note: Composite price index for agricultural goods refers to bananas, cocoa, coffee, copra, cotton, jute, rubber, tea and tropical logs. Non-agricultural goods are crude petroleum, copper and gold.
Source : OECD Secretariat calculation based on FAO and UNCTAD data.

Commodity markets remain volatile for a number of reasons. The rise in the price of coffee in 1994, sustained in 1995, was largely due to frost and drought conditions in Brazil, the world's largest coffee producing country. Brazil's production fell by almost 30 percent. In July 1995, many producing countries, united under the Association of Coffee Producing Countries, tried to influence prices by restricting their exports to 3.6 million tonnes of green beans in order to lift futures prices in the New York exchange to 180 US cents per pound. They did not achieve their goal, however, and the price of coffee fell by 25 percent in 1996 and an additional 18 percent in 1998.

LDCs' agricultural mono-exporters are also affected by changes in world consumption patterns. Both tea and coffee producer associations are looking to new markets in Russia and China to boost world demand. However, LDCs' exporters will not necessarily benefit from new market openings as they are not always in a competitive position vis-à-vis other exporters. Although their three primary export commodities account for 70 percent of their exports on average, LDCs rarely figure among the top ten world exporters of any commodity. Exceptions to this are some exporters of cotton (Mali and Sudan), jute (Bangladesh, Myanmar, Nepal) and tea (Bangladesh, Malawi and Tanzania). LDCs are decidedly price takers in fast-changing markets.

The role of multinational enterprises

Industrial organisation studies have suggested that changes in the organisational structure of commodity markets, namely the large presence of MNEs and cartels in the production and marketing of commodities, may have also contributed to the declining share of primary commodities in total trade. These studies show the final consumer markets for some commodities are dominated by few MNEs who control downstream marketing, transport and distribution. Thus, a few MNEs account for 85 percent or more of world trade in wheat, coffee, cocoa, grains, iron ore, jute, timber, tobacco and tea.

This raises two issues. On the one hand, the high costs associated with processing, packaging, advertising, marketing and distribution mean that the cost of primary commodities as a share of the processed product price is usually small. For example, for raw cotton, the growers' price represents about 4-8 percent of the final product price; for tobacco, this share is closer to 6 percent. For bananas, producer countries obtain about 14 percent of the retail price; for jute goods, it is 11-24 percent; for coffee, it is in the range of 12 to 25 percent. On the other hand, to the extent that the concentration of market power has led some MNEs to exert monopsony pressure on suppliers of primary commodities, this can partly explain the observed declining prices of primary commodities (and hence their declining share in world trade). Studies that have investigated this link have found little evidence to establish or to refute whether high concentration of market power exerted downward pressure on primary commodity prices.

Declining share of raw materials in world trade

In terms of the global pattern of trade in primary commodities, such trade has grown much more slowly than world GDP and has accounted for a declining share in world trade. In OECD countries, this share has fallen from 17 percent to 12 percent over the last 15 years; for all developing countries, the share has more than halved from 79 percent to 29 percent. This decline reflects the slower growth of world trade in commodities and the correspondingly higher growth in manufactures and services.

The major markets for most of these commodity producers are OECD countries where 65 percent of the world's commodity exports find their way, more or less in proportion to OECD countries' share in world GDP and world imports of manufactures. It is also worth noting that about half of the world's exports of primary commodities are accounted for by OECD countries, and this proportion has remained more or less the same over several decades. OECD countries dominate timber exports, where their share of total was 62 percent in 1995, vegetables (68%), energy (73%), tubers (75%), cereals (85%), and dairy products (89%). Developing countries dominate world markets in tobacco (52%), sugar (55%), coffee (79%), cocoa (69%), tea (80%), and rubber (98%).

Research that has investigated the factors that have led primary commodity trade to make up a declining share of world trade has identified two main causes: (1) low income elasticity of demand (mainly for food); and (2) declining intensity of raw materials use in economic activity.

Empirical evidence show an inverse relationship between consumption of primary commodities (mainly food) and incomes. Thus, in the United States, less than 10 percent of total personal expenditures is spent on food. For Canada, Japan, France, Australia, Italy, Hong Kong and Singapore, the share is between 10 and 20 percent. In India, food expenditures account for about 50 percent of total personal expenditures; in Mexico, where per capita incomes are significantly higher than in India, the share is closer to 37 percent. This suggests that the growth in demand for food will inevitably be slower than the growth in incomes.

In terms of consumption of raw materials, various studies have identified the following factors which work to restrain the growth of primary commodities below that in incomes: the evolution in the structure of economic activity in the key consuming countries towards products and services that require less material inputs; the development of synthetic substitutes, and a decline in the material intensity of industrial output generally.

One of the major uses for copper, for instance, the fifth largest LDCs' export product, has traditionally been copper wiring for telecommunications. Although telecommunications is a booming industry, demand for copper has not grown proportionally as technological advances have implied both raw material substitutes and less material intensity. Fibre optic cables are replacing copper wiring in traditional markets, and in new and expanding markets like China, cellular telephone capabilities account for the most dynamic growth in the industry.

Substitutes have also been found in the cobalt market. The cobalt market was traditionally influenced by the two producing countries, Congo (ex-Zaire) and Zambia. Cobalt is a by-product of the extensive Zairian and Zambian copper mining, but can also be mined as a by-product of nickel. Demand for cobalt, used primarily in the production of jet engines, has been ever rising. Since production has been unreliable from the two major producers in recent years due to political and other problems, nickel mining enterprises have started producing greater quantities of cobalt. In the future, the cobalt market will be shared between the two traditional producers, and in addition Canada, Cuba, Russia and Australia. The price of cobalt is projected to fall in 2-3 years as the new producers enter the market with full force.

Manufacturing sector in LDCs: small and sluggish

Another major impediment facing the majority of LDCs is the small size and lack of growth in their manufacturing sectors. The manufacturing sector in LDCs accounted for an average of only 11 percent of GDP in 1997, compared with 12 percent in 1980.

The manufacturing sector is under-developed in most LDCs due to extremely *low levels of investment* (20 percent of GDP in 1997). Few foreign, and indeed domestic investors are willing to take the risks implied in investing in countries with deficient regulatory environment, large infrastructure problems and often unstable economic or political environments. In 1997, FDI stock in GDP was 6 percent in LDCs as opposed to 17 percent in all developing countries (Appendix Table 1).

Appendix Table 1. Inward FDI stock in GDP

	1980	1985	1990	1995	1997
Developing countries (DC)	5.9	9.8	10.5	14.1	16.6
DCs minus China	6.4	11.0	11.1	13.4	15.5
LDCs	2.2	3.2	4.1	5.9	5.7
World total	5.0	6.9	8.7	9.9	11.7

Source : UNCTAD, *World Investment Report 1999*

LDCs' export markets

Appendix Table 2 shows the share of individual LDCs' exports to major regional destinations. The table shows LDCs' reliance on OECD markets is greater than the average for all developing countries, with their dependence on the EU market being especially important. OECD markets were the destination of some 63 percent of LDCs' exports in 1997. The EU represented the single most important outlet for LDCs' exports (32 percent), followed by the United States and Canada (23 percent) and Japan (4 percent). And the proportion of exports destined to OECD markets for 16 LDCs (Angola, Bangladesh, Cap Verde, Comoros, Congo, Gambia, Haiti, Madagascar, Mauritania, Niger, Samoa, Sao Tome and Principe, Sierra Leone, Uganda and Vanuatu) exceeded 80 percent in 1997. Overall, the share of LDCs' exports going to OECD markets is 9 percentage points higher than that for all developing countries. In addition, the share of LDCs' exports to other developing countries is 9 points lower than average. Therefore, it is evident that the conditions of market access to OECD countries are of critical importance in defining the trading opportunities of LDCs.

Appendix Table 2. Destinations of LDCs' exports, percentage shares in 1997

LDC	All OECD	European Union	Japan	USA & Canada	Other OECD	Eastern Europe	Developing Countries	Others
Afghanistan	46.2	31.5	6.3	7.4	1.0	6.7	47.1	0.0
Angola	80.7	14.6	0.1	64.9	1.1	0.0	17.6	1.7
Bangladesh	83.1	42.1	2.4	37.5	1.1	1.2	15.0	0.7
Benin	21.2	16.9	0.6	3.2	0.5	0.2	74.7	3.9
Burkina Faso	34.3	30.7	2.1	0.5	1.0	0.6	51.1	14.0
Burundi	63.8	48.8	0.0	0.9	14.1	0.0	1.6	34.6
Cambodia	26.4	11.2	1.0	13.9	0.3	0.5	73.1	0.0
Cape Verde	80.0	80.0	0.0	0.0	0.0	0.0	15.0	5.0
Central African Republic	48.6	47.5	0.3	0.6	0.2	2.9	14.3	34.2
Chad	50.2	45.2	1.6	2.9	0.5	1.8	42.3	5.7
Comoros	93.6	71.7	0.7	20.4	0.8	0.5	5.9	0.0
Dem. Republic of the	93.2	59.5	3.7	22.0	8.0	0.2	6.4	0.2
Djibouti	6.1	5.9	0.1	0.0	0.1	0.3	93.6	0.0
Equatorial Guinea	62.8	37.1	15.0	10.4	0.0	0.0	37.3	0.2
Ethiopia	77.3	50.8	11.2	13.3	2.0	4.7	16.8	1.2
Gambia	92.7	86.0	4.7	1.7	0.3	1.0	6.3	0.0
Guinea	56.0	39.0	0.4	14.4	2.2	27.8	15.9	0.3
Guinea-Bissau	15.7	14.4	0.8	0.3	0.2	0.0	83.6	0.7
Haiti	98.5	15.2	0.2	82.5	0.6	0.1	1.0	0.4
Kiribati	61.8	24.0	17.2	16.2	4.4	0.9	37.3	0.0
Laos	50.3	41.5	3.5	3.6	1.7	0.0	18.6	31.1
Liberia	69.4	48.0	0.0	0.5	20.9	17.2	13.4	0.0
Madagascar	86.6	69.1	5.8	10.3	1.4	0.9	11.8	0.7
Malawi	59.0	27.8	4.5	12.2	14.5	5.6	13.0	22.4
Maldives	62.4	22.4	18.7	21.0	0.3	0.3	35.1	2.2
Mali	40.2	31.5	1.0	5.2	2.5	0.2	46.2	13.4
Mauritania	84.8	59.9	24.5	0.1	0.3	1.2	13.2	0.8
Mozambique	71.2	35.4	8.1	12.4	15.3	1.1	23.6	4.1
Myanmar	31.8	12.2	7.7	10.9	1.0	0.1	52.5	15.6
Nepal	74.6	41.3	0.9	30.1	2.3	1.1	23.5	0.8
Niger	81.8	46.0	0.2	34.6	1.0	0.7	13.6	3.9
Rwanda	70.5	66.1	0.0	3.8	0.6	3.1	16.7	9.7
Samoa	87.3	7.3	1.3	7.2	71.5	2.9	6.7	3.1
Sao Tome and Principe	91.1	83.7	0.2	2.7	4.5	3.9	4.9	0.1
Sierra Leone	82.9	69.7	0.9	11.3	1.0	1.0	2.2	13.9
Solomon Islands	75.5	12.9	59.9	0.6	2.1	0.0	22.3	2.2
Somalia	13.4	13.3	0.0	0.1	0.0	0.2	86.4	0.0
Sudan	42.6	35.3	4.2	2.3	0.8	1.6	55.4	0.4
Togo	34.4	14.7	0.0	12.0	7.7	4.4	38.8	22.4
Uganda	82.9	71.9	0.7	7.2	3.1	10.0	6.6	0.5
United Republic of	46.6	33.1	7.5	3.9	2.1	2.6	44.3	6.5
Vanuatu	86.9	53.7	27.8	3.4	2.0	0.0	10.6	2.5
Yemen	19.4	8.1	5.3	0.3	5.7	0.0	80.2	0.4
Zambia	43.7	23.1	10.7	6.4	3.5	0.1	51.0	5.2
All LDCs	63.3	32.4	4.4	22.7	3.8	2.8	29.8	4.1
All developing countries	54.8	17.7	10.2	24.1	2.8	1.8	38.8	4.6

Source : UN COMTRADE database

APPENDIX 3.

Appendix Table 3. Classification of economies under various GSP programmes

	LDC (UN Definition)	Australian GSP	EU GSP	Japanese GSP	U.S. GSP
Afghanistan	ξ	θ	ξ	ξ	σ
Albania		σ	θ	θ	θ
Algeria		σ	θ	θ	—
American Samoa		σ	θ	θ	[1]
Angola	ξ	σ	ξ	ξ	ξ
Anguilla		σ	θ	?	θ
Antigua and Barbuda		σ	θ	θ	θ
Argentina		σ	θ	θ	θ
Armenia		?	θ	θ	θ
Aruba		?	θ	?	—
Azerbaijan		?	θ	θ	—
Bahamas		σ	θ	σ	σ
Bahrain		σ	θ	θ	θ
Baker Island		?	θ	?	[2]
Bangladesh	ξ	θ	ξ	ξ	ξ
Barbados		σ	θ	θ	θ
Belarus		?	θ	θ	σ
Belize		σ	θ	θ	θ
Benin	ξ	θ	ξ	ξ	ξ
Bermuda		σ	θ	σ	σ
Bhutan	ξ	θ	ξ	ξ	ξ
Bolivia		σ	+θ	θ	θ
Bosnia & Herzegovina		σ	[3]θ	?	θ
Botswana	[4]	θ	θ	θ	θ
Brazil		σ	θ	θ	θ
British Indian Ocean Territories		σ	θ	?	θ
British Virgin Islands		σ	θ	θ	θ
Brunei Darussalam		σ	θ	σ	σ
Bulgaria		σ	?	θ	θ
Burkina Faso	ξ	θ	ξ	ξ	ξ

ξ = Designated as a least-developed country.

θ = Developing country (WTO) or ordinary GSP status.

σ = Formerly held GSP status but have now been graduated, suspended, terminated or otherwise removed from the GSP.

— = Never designated to the GSP.

? = Unknown. Generally indicates that the country or territory is not currently designated for GSP benefits, but it is unclear whether it ever was in the past.

**θ = Australia grants preferences under the South Pacific Regional Trade and Economic Cooperation Agreement (SPARTECA).

+θ = Countries for which Article 7 of Council Regulation No. 2820/98 applies Article 7 grants further tariff reductions for countries that have made progress in the fight against drugs.

(continued)

(cont.)

	LDC (UN Definition)	Australian GSP	EU GSP	Japanese GSP	U.S. GSP
Burundi	ξ	θ	ξ	ξ	ξ
Cambodia	ξ	θ	ξ	ξ	ξ
Cameroon		σ	θ	θ	θ
Canary Islands		?	?	θ	—
Cape Verde	ξ	θ	ξ	ξ	ξ
Cayman Islands		σ	θ	σ	σ
Central African Rep.	ξ	θ	ξ	ξ	[5]ξ
Ceuta and Melilla		?	[6]	θ	—
Chad	ξ	θ	ξ	ξ	ξ
Chile		σ	θ	θ	[7]θ
China, Peoples Rep.		σ	θ	[8]θ	—
Chinese Taipei		σ	?	σ	σ
Christmas Island		[9]	θ	?	θ
Cocos (Keeling) Is.		[9]	θ	?	θ
Colombia		σ	+θ	θ	θ
Comoros	ξ	θ	ξ	?	ξ
Congo, Dem. Rep.		θ	ξ	θ	ξ
Congo, Republic of		σ	θ	θ	θ
Cook Islands[10]		θ	θ	θ	θ
Costa Rica		σ	+θ	θ	θ
Côte d'Ivoire		σ	θ	θ	θ
Croatia		σ	[3]θ	θ	θ
Cuba		σ	θ	θ	—
Cyprus		σ	θ	σ	σ
Czech Republic		σ	?	θ	θ
Djibouti	ξ	θ	ξ	?	ξ
Dominica		σ	θ	θ	θ
Dominican Republic		σ	θ	θ	θ
Ecuador		σ	+θ	θ	θ

ξ = Designated as a least-developed country.

θ = Developing country (WTO) or ordinary GSP status.

σ = Formerly held GSP status but have now been graduated, suspended, terminated or otherwise removed from the GSP.

— = Never designated to the GSP.

? = Unknown. Generally indicates that the country or territory is not currently designated for GSP benefits, but it is unclear whether it ever was in the past.

**θ = Australia grants preferences under the South Pacific Regional Trade and Economic Cooperation Agreement (SPARTECA).

+θ = Countries for which Article 7 of Council Regulation No. 2820/98 applies Article 7 grants further tariff reductions for countries that have made progress in the fight against drugs.

(continued)

(cont.)

	LDC (UN Definition)	Australian GSP	EU GSP	Japanese GSP	U.S. GSP
Egypt		σ	θ	θ	θ
El Salvador		σ	+θ	θ	θ
Equatorial Guinea	ξ	θ	ξ	ξ	ξ
Eritrea	ξ	σ	ξ	ξ	?
Estonia		?	?	θ	θ
Ethiopia	ξ	θ	ξ	ξ	[11] ξ
Falkland Islands		σ	θ	θ	θ
Fiji		**θ	θ	θ	θ
French Polynesia		σ	θ	θ	θ
Gabon		σ	θ	θ	θ
Gambia	ξ	θ	ξ	ξ	ξ
Georgia		?	θ	θ	—
Ghana		σ	θ	θ	θ
Gibraltar		σ	θ	θ	θ
Gilbert and Ellice Is.		σ	?	θ	σ
Greenland		?	θ	σ	—
Grenada		σ	θ	θ	θ
Guam		σ	θ	σ	[1]
Guatemala		σ	+θ	θ	θ
Guinea	ξ	θ	ξ	ξ	ξ
Guinea-Bissau	ξ	θ	ξ	ξ	ξ
Guyana		σ	θ	θ	θ
Haiti	ξ	θ	ξ	ξ	ξ
Heard & McDonald.		[9]	θ	?	θ
Honduras		σ	+θ	θ	θ
Hong Kong-China		σ	σ	σ	σ
Howland Island		?	θ	?	[2]
Hungary		σ	?	θ	θ
India		σ	θ	θ	θ
Indonesia		σ	θ	θ	θ

ξ = Designated as a least-developed country.

θ = Developing country (WTO) or ordinary GSP status.

σ = Formerly held GSP status but have now been graduated, suspended, terminated or otherwise removed from the GSP.

— = Never designated to the GSP.

? = Unknown. Generally indicates that the country or territory is not currently designated for GSP benefits, but it is unclear whether it ever was in the past.

**θ = Australia grants preferences under the South Pacific Regional Trade and Economic Cooperation Agreement (SPARTECA).

+θ = Countries for which Article 7 of Council Regulation No. 2820/98 applies Article 7 grants further tariff reductions for countries that have made progress in the fight against drugs.

(continued)

(cont.)

	LDC (UN Definition)	Australian GSP	EU GSP	Japanese GSP	U.S. GSP
Iran		σ	θ	θ	—
Iraq		σ	θ	θ	—
Israel		σ	?	σ	σ
Jamaica		σ	θ	θ	θ
Jarvis Island		?	θ	?	[2]
Jordan		σ	θ	θ	θ
Kazakhstan		?	θ	θ	θ
Kenya		σ	θ	θ	θ
Kingman Reef		?	θ	?	[1]
Kiribati	ξ	**θ	ξ	?	ξ
Korea, DPR	?	σ	?	?	—
Korea, Republic of		σ	σ	σ	σ
Kuwait		σ	θ	σ	—
Kyrgyzstan		?	θ	θ	θ
Lao PDR	ξ	θ	ξ	ξ	—
Latvia		?	?	θ	θ
Lebanon		σ	θ	θ	θ
Lesotho	ξ	θ	ξ	ξ	ξ
Liberia	ξ	θ	ξ	ξ	σ
Libya		σ	θ	θ	—
Lithuania		?	?	θ	θ
Macao		σ	θ	σ	σ
Macedonia, FYR		σ	[3]θ	θ	θ
Madagascar	ξ	θ	ξ	ξ	ξ
Malawi	ξ	θ	ξ	ξ	ξ
Malaysia		σ	θ	θ	σ
Maldives	ξ	θ	ξ	ξ	σ
Mali	ξ	θ	ξ	ξ	ξ
Malta		σ	?	θ	[12]θ
Marshall Islands		**θ	θ	θ	—

ξ = Designated as a least-developed country.

θ = Developing country (WTO) or ordinary GSP status.

σ = Formerly held GSP status but have now been graduated, suspended, terminated or otherwise removed from the GSP.

— = Never designated to the GSP.

? = Unknown. Generally indicates that the country or territory is not currently designated for GSP benefits, but it is unclear whether it ever was in the past.

**θ = Australia grants preferences under the South Pacific Regional Trade and Economic Cooperation Agreement (SPARTECA).

+θ = Countries for which Article 7 of Council Regulation No. 2820/98 applies Article 7 grants further tariff reductions for countries that have made progress in the fight against drugs.

(continued)

(cont.)

	LDC (UN Definition)	Australian GSP	EU GSP	Japanese GSP	U.S. GSP
Mauritania	ξ	θ	ξ	ξ	[13]ξ
Mauritius		σ	θ	θ	θ
Mayotte		?	θ	?	—
Mexico		σ	θ	θ	σ
Micronesia, Fed. States		**θ	θ	θ	—
Midway Island		σ	θ	?	[1]
Moldova		?	θ	θ	θ
Mongolia		σ	θ	θ	θ
Montserrat		σ	θ	θ	θ
Morocco		σ	θ	θ	θ
Mozambique	ξ	θ	ξ	ξ	ξ
Myanmar (Burma)	ξ	θ	[14]ξ	ξ	σ
Namibia		σ	θ	θ	θ
Nauru		**θ	θ	?	σ
Nepal	ξ	θ	ξ	ξ	ξ
Netherlands Antilles		σ	θ	σ	σ
New Caledonia		σ	θ	σ	θ
Nicaragua		σ	+θ	θ	[15]σ
Niger	ξ	θ	ξ	ξ	ξ
Nigeria		σ	θ	θ	θ
Niue Islands[10]		θ	θ	θ	θ
Norfolk Island		[9]	θ	?	θ
Oman		σ	θ	θ	θ
Pakistan		σ	θ	θ	θ
Palau		σ	θ	θ	σ
Palestinian Authority		σ	?	?	[16]
Palmyra Island		?	θ	?	[2]
Panama		σ	+θ	θ	θ

ξ = Designated as a least-developed country.

θ = Developing country (WTO) or ordinary GSP status.

σ = Formerly held GSP status but have now been graduated, suspended, terminated or otherwise removed from the GSP.

— = Never designated to the GSP.

? = Unknown. Generally indicates that the country or territory is not currently designated for GSP benefits, but it is unclear whether it ever was in the past.

**θ = Australia grants preferences under the South Pacific Regional Trade and Economic Cooperation Agreement (SPARTECA).

+θ = Countries for which Article 7 of Council Regulation No. 2820/98 applies Article 7 grants further tariff reductions for countries that have made progress in the fight against drugs.

(continued)

(cont.)

	LDC (UN Definition)	Australian GSP m	EU GSP	Japanese GSP	U.S. GSP
Papua New Guinea		[17]θ	θ	θ	θ
Paraguay		σ	θ	θ	[18]θ
Peru		σ	+θ	θ	θ
Philippines		σ	θ	θ	θ
Pitcairn Island		σ	θ	?	θ
Poland		σ	?	θ	θ
Qatar		σ	θ	?	—
Romania		σ	σ	θ	[19]θ
Russia		?	θ	?	θ
Rwanda	ξ	θ	ξ	ξ	ξ
Samoa	ξ	**θ	ξ	ξ	?
Sao Tome & Principe	ξ	θ	ξ	ξ	ξ
Saudi Arabia		σ	θ	θ	—
Senegal		σ	θ	θ	θ
Seychelles		σ	θ	θ	θ
Sierra Leone	ξ	θ	ξ	θ	ξ
Singapore		σ	σ	σ	σ
Slovakia		σ	?	θ	θ
Slovenia		σ	?	θ	θ
Solomon Islands	ξ	θ	ξ	ξ	θ
Somalia	ξ	θ	ξ	ξ	ξ
South Africa		?	θ	θ	θ
Sri Lanka		σ	θ	θ	θ
St. Helena		σ	θ	θ	θ
St. Kitts and Nevis		[20]σ	θ	θ	θ
St. Lucia		σ	θ	θ	θ
St. Pierre & Miquelon		σ	θ	?	—
St. Vincent & Grens.		σ	θ	θ	θ
Sudan	ξ	θ	ξ	ξ	σ
Suriname		σ	θ	θ	θ
Swaziland		σ	θ	θ	θ

ξ = Designated as a least-developed country.

θ = Developing country (WTO) or ordinary GSP status.

σ = Formerly held GSP status but have now been graduated, suspended, terminated or otherwise removed from the GSP.

— = Never designated to the GSP.

? = Unknown. Generally indicates that the country or territory is not currently designated for GSP benefits, but it is unclear whether it ever was in the past.

**θ = Australia grants preferences under the South Pacific Regional Trade and Economic Cooperation Agreement (SPARTECA).

+θ = Countries for which Article 7 of Council Regulation No. 2820/98 applies Article 7 grants further tariff reductions for countries that have made progress in the fight against drugs.

(continued)

(cont.)

	LDC (UN Definition)	Australian GSP	EU GSP	Japanese GSP	U.S. GSP
Syrian Arab Republic		σ	θ	θ	σ
Tajikistan		?	θ	θ	—
Tanzania	ξ	θ	ξ	ξ	ξ
Thailand		σ	θ	θ	θ
Togo	ξ	θ	ξ	ξ	ξ
Tokelau Islands[10]		**θ	θ	θ	θ
Tonga		**θ	θ	θ	θ
Trinidad and Tobago		σ	θ	θ	θ
Tunisia		σ	θ	θ	θ
Turkey		σ	?	θ	θ
Turkmenistan		?	θ	θ	—
Turks & Caicos Is.		σ	θ	θ	θ
Tuvalu	ξ	**θ	ξ	?	ξ
Uganda	ξ	θ	ξ	ξ	ξ
Ukraine		?	θ	θ	θ
United Arab Emirates		σ	θ	σ	—
Uruguay		σ	θ	θ	θ
U.S. Virgin Islands		σ	θ	σ	1
Uzbekistan		?	θ	θ	θ
Vanuatu	ξ	**θ	ξ	ξ	ξ
Venezuela		σ	+θ	θ	θ
Viet Nam		σ	θ	θ	—
Wake Island		σ	θ	?	1
Wallis and Futuna		σ	θ	?	θ
West Bank & Gaza		?	?	θ	θ
Western Sahara		?	?	?	θ
Western Samoa		?	?	?	θ
Yemen	ξ	θ	ξ	ξ	ξ
Yugoslavia, Fed. Rep.		?	?	θ	—
Yugoslavia, the former		σ	?	θ	σ
Zambia	ξ	θ	ξ	ξ	ξ
Zimbabwe		σ	θ	θ	θ

ξ = Designated as a least-developed country.

θ = Developing country (WTO) or ordinary GSP status.

σ = Formerly held GSP status but have now been graduated, suspended, terminated or otherwise removed from the GSP.

— = Never designated to the GSP.

? = Unknown. Generally indicates that the country or territory is not currently designated for GSP benefits, but it is unclear whether it ever was in the past.

**θ = Australia grants preferences under the South Pacific Regional Trade and Economic Cooperation Agreement (SPARTECA).

+θ = Countries for which Article 7 of Council Regulation No. 2820/98 applies Article 7 grants further tariff reductions for countries that have made progress in the fight against drugs.

Notes

1 A U.S. insular possession.

2 Part of American Oceania.

3 Preferential treatment is limited to specified agricultural products in chapters 1-24.

4 Botswana was originally designated as an LDC in 1971, but was graduated from this status in 1994.

5 The Central African Republic was suspended from the U.S. GSP scheme in 1988, and reinstated in 1990.

6 Part of Spain.

7 Chile was suspended from the U.S. GSP scheme in 1988, and reinstated in 1991.

8 Excluding Hong Kong and Macao.

9 Part of Australian Oceania.

10 Part of New Zealand Oceania.

11 Ethiopia was suspended from the U.S. GSP scheme in 1978, and reinstated in 1992.

12 Malta and Gozo.

13 Mauritania was suspended from the U.S. GSP scheme in 1993, and reinstated in 1999.

14 The EU has suspended Myanmar's GSP benefits since April 1997 due to human rights violations. See Council Regulation (EC) No 552/97 of 24 March 1997.

15 Nicaragua was removed from the GSP in 1987, but now receives benefits under the Caribbean Basin Initiative.

16 Treated as part of the U.S.-Israel free trade area.

17 Australia grants preferences under the Papua New Guinea Agreement.

18 Paraguay was suspended from the U.S. GSP scheme in 1987, and reinstated in 1991.

19 Romania was removed from the U.S. GSP scheme in 1987, and reinstated in 1994.

20 Listed as St. Christopher and Nevis

BIBLIOGRAPHY

Abramovitz, M. and P. David, (1996), "Convergence and Deferred Catch-up: Productivity Leadership and the Waning of American Exceptionalism," in The Mosaic of Economic Growth' by Landau, Ralph; Taylor, Timothy and Wright, Gavin, Stanford University Press: California, pp 21-62.

Ades, A. and R. Di Tella, (1997), "National Champions and Corruption: Some Unpleasant Interventionist Arithmetic," Economic Journal, (July 2000), Vol. 107, pp. 1023-1042.

Ades, A. and R. Di Tella, (1999), "Rents, Competition and Corruption,"American Economic Review, (September 1999) Vol. 89, no. 4, pp. 982-993.

Aghion, P., E. Caroli, and C. Garcia-Penasola, (1999), "Inequality and Economic Growth: The Perspective of the New Growth Theories," *Journal of Economic Literature*, 37(4), December 1999, pages 1615-60.

Amsden, A. (1989), "Asia's next giant: South Korea and late industrialization" New York and Oxford: Oxford University Press.

Balassa, B., (1985), "Exports, Policy Choices, and Economic Growth in Developing Countries after the 1973 Oil Shock," Journal of Development Economics, vol. 18(2), pp. 23-35.

Benabou, R. (1996), "Inequality and Growth,"in B. Bernanke and J. Rotemberg, eds, *National Bureau of Economic Research Macroeconomics Annual*. Cambridge, Mass.: MIT Press.

Bigstein, (2000), "Globalisation and Income Inequality in Uganda," prepared for OECD conference on Poverty and Income Inequality in Developing Countries: A Policy Dialogue on the Effects of Globalisation (30 Nov - 1 Dec 2000).

Chadha, R. (1999a) "Trade, Technology and Employment: Some Missing Links in India's Rural Economy," *Indian Journal of Labour-Economics*; 42(4), Oct.-Dec. 1999, pages 881-908.

Chadha, R. (1999b), "*GATS and Developing Countries: A Case Study of India,*" National Center for Advanced Economic Research, New Delhi, *mimeo*.

Chadha et al., (2000) "Developing Countries and the Next Round of WTO Negotiations," *World Economy*; 23(4), April 2000, pages 431-36.

Clague, C. et al, (1997), "Institutions and Economic Development: Growth and Governance in Less-Developed and Post-Socialist Countries", The John Hopkins University Press, Baltimore, Maryland.

Coe, D, E. Helpman, and A. W. Hoffmaister, (1997), "North-South R&D Spillovers," *Economic Journal*, 107, pp. 134-149.

Coe, D, E. Helpman, and A. W. Hoffmaister, (1995), "International R&D Spillovers," *European Economic Review*, 39, pp. 859-887.

Crafts, N. (2000), "Globalisation and Growth in the Twentieth Century," IMF Working Paper no. 00/44, March 2000.

De la Cuadra, S. and D. Hachette, (1991), "Chile," Part II of Papageorgiou D., Michaely M. and Choksi A. *Liberalising Foreign Trade*, Volume I, Blackwell, Oxford.

Dean, J., S. Desai and J. Reidel, (1994), "Trade Policy Reform in Developing Countries Since 1985: A Review of the Evidence," World Bank Discussion Paper no. 267.

Deardorff, A. (1999), *"International Provision of Trade Services, Trade and Fragmentation,"* Ann Arbor: University of Michigan, *mimeo*.

Doig, A. and S. Riley's, (1998), 'Corruption and anti-corruption strategies: issues and case studies from developing countries', Chapter 3 of UNDP *Corruption & Integrity Improvement Initiatives in Developing Countries*, Paris 1997, pp.45-62.

Dollar, D. (1992), "Outward-Oriented Developing Economies Really Do Grow More Rapidly: Evidence from 95 LDCs, 1976-1985," *Economic Development and Cultural Change*; 40(3), April 1992, pages 523-44.

Dollar, D. and A. Kraay, (2000), "Trade, Growth and Poverty", Development Research Group, World Bank. Prepared for the conference on 'Poverty and the International Economy' sponsored by the Swedish Ministry of Foreign Affairs, the William Davidson Institute and the World Bank, October 20-21, Stockholm, Sweden.

Edwards, S. (1998), "Openness, Trade Liberalization, and Growth in Developing Countries", Milner,-Chris, ed. *Developing and newly industrializing countries.* Volume 1. *Globalization of the World Economy*, vol. 4. Cheltenham, U.K. and Northampton, Mass.: Elgar; distributed by American International Distribution Corporation Williston, Vt., 1998, pages 39-74.

Edwards, S. and D. Lederman, (1999), "The Political Economy of Unilateral Trade Liberalisation: The Case of Chile,"NBER Working Paper no. 6510, April 1998.

Esfahani, H.S., (1991), "Exports, Imports and Economic Growth in Semi-Industrialised Countries," *Journal of Development Economics;* vol. 35, pp. 93-116.

Feenstra, R.C., Madani, D., Tzu-Han, Y., and Chi-Yuan, L., (1997), "Testing Endogenous Growth in South Korea and Taiwan," NBER Working Paper No. 6028.

Fernandez, R.C. and R. Portes, (1998), "Returns to Regionalsim: An Analysis of Nontraditional Gains from Regional Trade Agreements," World Bank Economic Review, Vol. 12, no. 2, pp. 197-220.

Fernandez, R.C. and D. Rodrik, (1991), "Resistance to Reform: Status Quo Bias in the Presence of Individual-Specific Uncertainty," *American-Economic-Review*; 81(5), December 1991, pages 1146-55.

Finger, M., H. Hall and D. Nelson (1982), "The Political Economy of Administered Protection,*"American Economic Review*, 72(3), June 1982, pages 452-66.

Finger, M. (1981), "Policy Research," *Journal of Political Economy* , 89, pages 581-589.

Findlay, C. and T. Warren, eds. (2000*), Impediments to Trade in Services: Measurement and Policy Implications*, Sydney: Routledge.

Francois, J. and B. Hoekman, (1999), "*Market Access in the Services Sectors,*" Washington, D.C.: The World Bank, *mimeo.*

Francois, J. and I. Wooton (1999), "*Trade in International Transport Services: The Role of Competition*", Tinbergen Institute, Erasmus University, Rotterdam, *mimeo.*

Francois, J.F., B.J. McDonald, and H. Nordstrom, (1995), "Assessing the Uruguay Round," in *The Uruguay Round and the Developing Economies*, edited by W. Martin and L.A. Winters, Washington: World Bank (discussion paper number 307), 1995

Frankel, J. and D. Romer, (1999), "Does Trade Cause Growth?" *American Economic Review*, (June), Vol. 89, no. 3, pp. 379-399.

Gatti, R. (1999), "Corruption and Trade Tariffs, or a Case for Uniform Tariffs," Policy Research Working Paper 2216, World Bank Development Research Group, Washington, D.C.

Harrison, A. (1996), "Openness and Growth: A Time-Series Cross-Country Analysis for Developing Countries," Journal of Development Economics, vol. 48, pp. 419-447.

Harrison, A. et al., (1995), "The Effects of Trade Policy Reform: What Do We Really Know?," National Bureau of Economic Research Working Paper: 5225.

Heeks, R., 1998, "The Uneven Profile of Indian Software Exports,"*Development Informatics Working Paper* No. 3, Institute for Development Policy and Management, University of Manchester.

Hoekman, B. and D. Konan, (1999), "Deep Integration, Non-Discrimination and Euro-Mediterranean Free Trade." Centre for Economic Policy Research Discussion Paper: 2095.

Hoekman, B. and A. Mattoo, (1999), "Services, Economic Development and the Next Round of Negotiations on Services," Washington, D.C.: The World Bank, mimeo.

ILO, (1998), Country Studies on the Social Impact of Globalisation, Task Force on Country Studies on Globalisation, International Labour Office, Geneva, various country studies.

Irwin, D. (2000), Tariffs and Growth in Late Nineteenth Century America, NBER Working Paper No. W7639.

Jonsson, G. and A. Subramanian, (1999) "Dynamic Gains from Trade - Evidence from South Africa" IMF Working Paper WP/00/45.

Kaufmann, D. (1998), "Revisiting anti-corruption strategies: tilt towards incentive-driven approaches," Chapter 4 of UNDP *Corruption & Integrity Improvement Initiatives in Developing Countries*, Paris 1997, pp.63-82.

Keller, W. (1999), "How Trade Patterns and Technology Flows Affect Productivity Growth," NBER Working Paper 6990.

Kpundeh, S. (1998), "Political will in fighting corruption," Chapter 6 of UNDP *Corruption & Integrity Improvement Initiatives in Developing Countries*, Paris 1997, pp.91-110.

Krueger, A. (1978), "Liberalisation Attempts and Consequences" "Liberalisation, Direction of Bias and Economic Growth" (ch 12) in *Foreign Trade Regimes and Economic Development* , Volume X, NBER, New York, Ch 12, pp 277-300.

Krueger, A. (1990), "Asian Trade and Growth Lessons," AEA Papers and Proceedings (May 1990), in *Lessons for Development from the Experience in Asia*, Vol. 80, no.2, pp. 108-111.

Mattoo, A., (1999a), "*Developing Countries in the New Round of GATS Negotiations: From a Defensive to a Proactive Role*", Washington, D.C.: The World Bank, (March), *mimeo.*

Mattoo, A., (1999b), "Financial Services and the World Trade Organisation: Liberalisation Commitments of the Developing and Transition Economies," World Bank Working Papers No, 2184, Washington, D.C.

Mosley, P. (2000), "Globalisation, Economic Policy and Convergence" in *World-Economy*; 23(5), May 2000, pages 613-34.

Nguyen, T. et al., (1993), "An Evaluation of the Draft Final Act of the Uruguay Round" in *Economic-Journal*; 103(421), November 1993, pages 1540-49.

Palley, T. (1999), "The Economic Case for International Labour Standards: Theory and Evidence." American Federation of Labour and Congress of International Organisation)AFL-CIO), Washington, D.C.

Rodriguez, F. and D. Rodrik, (1999), "Trade Policy and Economic Growth: A Skeptic's Guide to the Cross-National Evidence," University of Maryland, Department of Economics, College Park.

Rodrik, D. (1996), "Labour Standards in International Trade: Do They Matter and What Do We Do About Them?," in R. Lawrence, D. Rodrik, and J. Whalley, eds., Emerging Agenda for Global Trade: High Stakes for Developing Countries. Policy Essay 20. Washington, D.C.: Overseas Development Council.

Rodrik, D. (1997), "Trade Policy and Economic Performance in Sub-Saharan Africa." Harvard University, J.F.K. School of Government, Cambridge, Mass.

Rodrik, D. (1998), "Where Did All the Growth Go? External Shocks, Social Conflict, and Growth Collapses," NBER Working Paper no. 6350, (January 1998) /Journal of Economic Growth, Vol. 4, no.4.

Rodrik, D. (1999a), "Institutions for High-Quality Growth: What They Are and How To Acquire Them." Paper presented at the International Monetary Fund conference on second generation reforms, 8-9 November Washington, D.C.

Rodrik, D. (1999b), "The New Global Economy and Developing Countries: Making Openess Work." Policy Essay 24. Washington, D.C.: Overseas Development Council.

Rodrik, D. (2000), "Institutions for High-Quality Growth: What They Are And How to Acquire Them,"NBER Working Paper no. 7540 (February 2000), Cambridge, Mass.

Rogers and Swinnerton, (2000), "The Economics of Child Labor: Comment," *American Economic Review*; 89(5), December 1999, pages 1382-85.

Romer, P. (1993), "Openess and Inflation: Theory and Evidence," *Quarterly Journal of Economics*, vol. 108, Issue 4 (November 1993), pp. 870-903.

Ruggiero, R. (1998), *"Towards GATS 2000 – a European Strategy,"* Address to the Conference on Trade in Services organized by the European Commission, Brussels (2 June).

Sachs, J., and A.M. Warner, (1995), "Economic Growth and the Process of Global Integration," *Brookings Papers on Economic Activity*, pp. 1 -95.

Srinivasan, T.N. and J. Bhagwati, (1999), "Outward Orientation and Development: Are Revisionists Right?," Center Discussion Paper no. 806, September 1999.

Stasavage, D. and C. Daubree's, (1997), "The determinants of Customs Fraud: Evidence from Senegal and Mali," paper at the UNDP-OECD Development Centre Conference on Corruption & Integrity Improvement Initiatives in Developing Countries, Paris 1997.

Tybout, J. (2000), "Manufacturing Firms in Developing Countries: How Well Do They Do, and Why?" in *Journal-of-Economic-Literature*; 38(1), March 2000, pages 11-44.

Vamvakidis, A. (1998), " Regional Trade Agreements Versus Broad Liberalization: Which Path Leads to Faster Growth? Time-Series Evidence" in International Monetary Fund Working Paper: WP/98/40, March 1998, pages 34.

Wei, S. (2000), "Natural Openess and Good Government," NBER Working Paper no. 7765 (June 2000).

Winters, L.A., (2000), "Trade Liberalisation and Poverty," Discussion Paper No. 7, Poverty Research Unit, Sussex, University of Sussex, UK.

World Bank (1997), Global Economic Prospects and Developing Countries, Washington, D.C.

World Bank, (2000), "Corruption in Bangladesh: Costs and Cures," The World Bank, Washington, D.C.

World Bank Data, "2000 World Development Indicators", The World Bank, Washington, D.C.

Yeats, A. (1997), "Just How Big is Global Production Sharing?," Background Paper prepared for Global Economic Prospects 1997. World Bank, Washnington, D.C.

GLOSSARY

ATC	Agreement on Textiles and Clothing
DAC	Development Assistance Committee (OECD)
FDI	Foreign direct investment
GATS	General Agreement on Trade in Services
GATT	General Agreement on Tariffs and Trade
GDP	Gross domestic product
GSP	Generalised System of Preferences
ILO	International Labour Organisation
IMF	International Monetary Fund
LDCs	Least developed countries
MFA	Multifibre Arrangement
MFN	Most-favoured nation
MNE	Multinational enterprise
MTN	Multilateral trade negotiation
MTS	Multilateral trading system
NGO	Non-governmental organisation
NTB	Non-tariff barrier
PSI	Pre-shipment inspection
QR	Quantitative restriction
S&D	Special and differential treatment
SPS	Sanitary and phytosanitary measure
SSA	Sub-Saharan Africa
TBT	Technical barrier to trade
TRIMs	Trade-related investment measures
TRIPS	Trade-related aspects of intellectual property rights
UNCTAD	United Nations Conference on Trade and Development
UNEP	United Nations Environment Programme
USTR	US Trade Representative
WTO	World Trade Organisation

OECD PUBLICATIONS, 2, rue André-Pascal, 75775 PARIS CEDEX 16
PRINTED IN FRANCE
(22 2001 06 1 P) ISBN 92-64-19675-7 – No. 52235 2001